THE CONTEMPORARY HISTORY OF DRUG-BASED ORGANISED CRIME IN SCOTLAND

EMERALD ADVANCES IN HISTORICAL CRIMINOLOGY

Series Editors: David Churchill and Christopher W. Mullins

This series embraces a broad, pluralistic understanding of 'the historical' and its potential applications to criminology. Providing an inclusive platform for a range of approaches which, in various ways, seek to orient criminological enquiry to history or to the dynamics of historical time, the series also offers a platform both for conventional studies in the history of crime and criminal justice but also for innovative and experimental work which extends the conceptual, theoretical, methodological and topical range of historical criminology. In this way, the series encourages historical scholarship on non-traditional topics in criminology (such as environmental harms, war and state crime) and inventive modes of theorising and practising historical research (including processual approaches and futures research). The series thus makes a valuable contribution to criminology irrespective of disciplinary affiliation, theoretical framing or methodological practice.

Previous Titles

History & Crime: A Transdisciplinary Approach edited by Thomas J. Kehoe and Jeffrey E. Pfeifer

The First British Crime Survey: An Ethnography of Criminology Within Government by Julian Molina

A Socio-Legal History of the Laws of War: Constraining Carnage by Christopher W. Mullins

A Socio-Legal History of the Laws of War: The Birth of International Humanitarian Law by Christopher W. Mullins

Politics and Public Protection by Mike Nash and Andy Williams

THE CONTEMPORARY HISTORY OF DRUG-BASED ORGANISED CRIME IN SCOTLAND

BY

ROBERT MCLEAN
University of the West of Scotland, UK

CHRIS HOLLIGAN
University of the West of Scotland, UK

and

MICHAEL PUGH
University of the West of Scotland, UK

United Kingdom – North America – Japan – India
Malaysia – China

Emerald Publishing Limited
Emerald Publishing, Floor 5, Northspring, 21-23 Wellington Street, Leeds LS1 4DL

First edition 2024

Copyright © 2024 Robert McLean, Chris Holligan and Michael Pugh.
Published under exclusive licence by Emerald Publishing Limited.

Reprints and permissions service
Contact: www.copyright.com

No part of this book may be reproduced, stored in a retrieval system, transmitted in any form or by any means electronic, mechanical, photocopying, recording or otherwise without either the prior written permission of the publisher or a licence permitting restricted copying issued in the UK by The Copyright Licensing Agency and in the USA by The Copyright Clearance Center. Any opinions expressed in the chapters are those of the authors. Whilst Emerald makes every effort to ensure the quality and accuracy of its content, Emerald makes no representation implied or otherwise, as to the chapters' suitability and application and disclaims any warranties, express or implied, to their use.

British Library Cataloguing in Publication Data
A catalogue record for this book is available from the British Library

ISBN: 978-1-83549-653-4 (Print)
ISBN: 978-1-83549-652-7 (Online)
ISBN: 978-1-83549-654-1 (Epub)

Printed and bound by CPI Group (UK) Ltd, Croydon, CR0 4YY

INVESTOR IN PEOPLE

CONTENTS

Acknowledgements vii

Prologue: The Applerow Atrocity ix

1. Introduction — 1
2. Pinning Down Organised Crime: Literature Review — 13
3. The Illegal Drug Trade in West Scotland — 31
4. Gang Reorganisation Around Drug Networks, 1980–1994 — 47
5. The 1995–1998 Drug Wars — 61
6. History Repeats Itself in North Glasgow — 77
7. Conclusion and Policy Lessons — 89

References 105

ACKNOWLEDGEMENTS

I would like to thank God for the blessings He has given myself: a loving family and amazing experiences. I would also like to thank my colleagues, peers and MRes supervision team including Prof Jim Mills and Prof Arthur McIvor. Furthermore, I would also like to take this opportunity to thank Professor James Densley, Professor Simon Harding, Professor Ross Deuchar and Professor Chris Holligan, who have all been instrumental in helping me achieve my academic goals, publications and with general career advice. I would also like to thank my colleagues, Dr Rajeev Gundur and Dr Colin Atkinson, who have helped offer career guidance. To everyone, thank you.

Robert McLean

I would like to thank Dr Robert McLean for his superb initiative and drive and for involving me in this exciting project. Also, I wish to acknowledge my two friends and former neighbours Guy and Dave of Tenbury Wells whose positive 'can do' outlooks inspire and motivate.

Chris Holligan

I'm grateful to Robert and Chris for the opportunity to contribute to finalising this book project with them, and to my wife and children (and our cat) for tolerating me in the process.

Michael Pugh

PROLOGUE: THE APPLEROW ATROCITY

On a chilly Wednesday afternoon, shortly before 2:12 p.m. on 6 December 2006, a blue Mazda car, registration S733ESF, was captured on CCTV parked outside the Applerow Motors MOT garage in Glasgow's Lambhill Estate. The garage is a family run business, owned by David Lyons, brother of Eddie Lyons senior, known figurehead of the Lyons crime family, based in Milton, Glasgow. Stepping out from the Mazda, two men disguised with 'old man' masks and trench coats, later identified as Raymond 'Rainbow' Anderson, then 45, and James Scott McDonald, then 33, proceeded to enter the garage forecourt, armed with military grade firearms, as the workers inside went about their business of testing and repairing motor vehicles (Scottish Courts & Tribunals, 2022, p. 6). It is believed that Raymond's son, Junior, was also present during the time of the incident, as the driver of the Mazda, though charges against him were dropped at the subsequent court trail. Among those working inside the garage were David Lyons, his son Mark and his nephew Michael Lyons Junior. David's nephew, Steven Lyons, accompanied by his friend, Robert 'Piggy' Pickett, the gunmen's intended targets, were also present. Steven's vehicle, a Ford Focus, was booked in to be serviced that day.

David Lyons was first to spot the masked pair. He called out a warning to the others inside. His nephew, Michael Junior, took heed and attempted to flee; however, one of the gunmen would fatally wound him with a single shot through the chest (Scottish Courts & Tribunals, 2022). Steven Lyons, at the time of his uncle's warning call, was seated in his vehicle. Steven instinctively slammed on the accelerator as a bullet shattered the Focus's rear window. Having nowhere to go, the vehicle struck the metal perimeter fence, bringing it to a halt. A second bullet was then fired, superficially striking Steven on the back. A third, and final shot in his direction, would result in a bullet passing through his leg, breaking it in two in the process, as he attempted to flee from the smashed vehicle for more adequate cover (Findlay, 2012a). Pickett was less lucky than Steven and received considerably worse injuries. As the masked pair entered the garage, Pickett had been standing outside the vehicle. Trapped inside the small unit, he was an easy target. Soon, Pickett was shot twice in the back, before one of the gunmen pumped a third bullet into his abdomen from close range, only two feet away (Findlay, 2012a, p. 88). The gunmen then proceeded to run back to the Mazda car, get in and drive off. The car was found two days later on Friday, 8th December 2006, abandoned in Vaila Street, Cadder, a short distance from the *locus*, having been set alight and burned out. The attack took all of three minutes. By 2:15 p.m., two men lay critically ill, while a third, Michael Junior, was dead (Scottish Courts & Tribunals, 2011).

1

INTRODUCTION

Although it reads as a storyline straight from a Hollywood movie script, the Applerow incident hammered home to the Scottish Government, Police Scotland and other stakeholders involved in the country's criminal justice apparatus, the stark reality of, and serious threat posed by, drug-based organised crime in Scotland. For a variety of reasons, extending to multiple facets of society, prior to the 'Applerow massacre', Scotland's illicit drugs trade had grown exponentially in just over 10 years. Any strategic response from those in positions of power tended to be laissez faire, ad hoc and operationalised in a desultory fashion. As a result, the illicit drug market grew almost unchecked (Deuchar et al., 2021). While drug harms had skyrocketed since the heroin boom, in the late 80s, as did ensuing violence, since the mid-90s, the government had been all too aware that the US federal 'war on drugs', initiated under the Nixon administration in 1971, had proven a costly and highly criticised disaster in the States. Halting the drugs trade in Scotland, given it was driven by socio-economic supply–demand processes, characterised by a multiplicity of persistent and intersecting factors, would prove extremely difficult.

Attempting to tackle gun violence directly related to drug-based organised crime at its root could prove a beartrap for any political party willing to accept the challenge. The Applerow shootings, however, signalled an escalation in violence associated with drug-based organised crime in the city. The incident drew considerable attention from newspapers, printing numerous back-to-back stories, uncovering the true extent, and fearful grip that drug-based organised crime had on Scotland's west coast. This movement to report on drug-based organised crime was spearheaded by then investigative journalist, turned Conservative MSP (2021–), Russell Findlay. Findlay's centre spread *'would you let this man look after your children?'*, for the Daily Record, shed light on the growing feud between criminal fraternities in Northern Glasgow, namely the Lyons and Daniels crime families (2012a). The piece named key actors, and listing a series of tit-for-tat assaults, stabbings and shootings that had occurred with increasing frequency on the streets of Glasgow, prior to Applerow, highlighting a marked increase in danger to the wider public [Eddie Lyons Senior, who ran a crimogenic youth club, discussed in chapter 6].

Related campaigns from community groups and partnerships had long recognised, and now sought to expose, the ever-increasing threats an illicit drugs market posed to wider public safety, while contributing to the sustained erosion of community life. The Glasgow public, as voiced by SNP councillor (Canal Ward) Billy McAllister, who had been elected in 2006 on the pledge of bringing drug-based organised crime to the attention of the Scottish Parliament at Holyrood and the UK Parliament at Westminster, had had enough. He demanded an effective government response to a worsening crisis (UK Parliament, 2006). McAllister was subsequently given bodyguards for his own protection, after a £50,000 contract was put on his head for speaking out publicly. In less than 6 months, in May 2007, the Scottish National Party (SNP) replaced Scottish Labour at the helm of Scotland's devolved government. Alex Salmond would replace Labour's Jack McConnell as Scotland's First Minister. Eager to make an impact, perhaps an overzealous SNP, publicly acknowledged the problem and within a year published *'The Road to Recovery: A New Approach to Tackling Scotland's Drug Problem'*, indicating a desire to create a 'drug free Scotland' within 10 years (Scottish government, 2008). While overblown, this statement of intent had been supported by earlier action. In October 2007, the country's first dedicated Serious Organised Crime Taskforce (SOCT) came into being. Its purpose: to eradicate the illegal drugs trade flourishing in the country. In an era of continued adherence to new public management principles, focusing on performance measurement, the SOCT was a bold, yet potentially risky, declaration. Yet, supported by an intelligible strategic overview, as indicated in subsequent government publications in 2009, 2015 and 2016, and the creation of an Anglo-Welsh counterpart in 2013, in the form of the National Crime Agency (NCA), it was a welcomed addition, as a tool at Police Scotland's disposal to address the growing menace that is drug-based organised crime (NCA, 2013; Scottish government, 2009, 2015, 2016).

Before the year 2000 and a United Nations conference – The Palermo Convention (2000), which followed that same year – the term 'organised crime' was rarely, if ever, used by politicians or law enforcement in the European context. When the term was used, it was typically without any degree of agreed consensus, consistency or background. The same proved even truer in the UK context where law enforcement had not even considered the possibility of organised crime as a plausible phenomenon on British shores. Organised crime was a US concept, particular to the States and affiliated with Mafia organisations with international ties, with preindustrial origins rooted the Sicilian Cosa Nostra, thus ultimately alien to Britain. In the United Kingdom, criminals operated, somewhat strictly, in illicit markets, and utilised specialist skill sets, for typically acquiring financial rewards, and as such were simply deemed 'professional criminals' (Von Lampe, 2016). The term professional was used as an adjective indicating a skill set honed by experienced criminals. The term was also applied at the individual level, neglecting differences when situated within the group context. Before the late 1980s, professional criminals were almost exclusively involved in predatory-based crimes: characterised as loosely coordinated, yet planned, attacks which occurred in short, intense, durations (McLean, 2019a, 2019b, 2019c). This included activities like armed robbery, kidnap/ransom, bank robberies, safe cracking and jewellery heists. The Great Train robbery, involving the now infamous professional criminal Ronnie Briggs, embodies the point eloquently (Hobbs & Antonopoulos, 2013).

The Palermo Convention, launched by US think tanks, resulted in the extrapolation of not only the term organised crime but also to its adoption as an analytical lens and policy preoccupation globally. The United States would prompt nations who signed the Convention to accept organised crime as a very real concept, permeating their national borders. Since the 1980s and 1990s, the end of the Cold War, coinciding with strategic free market policies, had helped accelerate the capitalisation of the global economy. Subsequently, as the legitimate international market expanded across the globe, with trade increasing, and profits surging, the illegal market mirrored this success. Consequently, market-based crime largely replaced predatory-based criminality; more so given post-war advances in technology, the implementation of methodical transportation systems, the professionalisation of security and the digitalisation of money, which simultaneously impacted upon the success rates of predatory-based criminality. The drug trade was one such market. Following the ebb and flow of the cannabis and cocaine trade, the heroin boom in the late 1980s had a particularly devastating effect on communities, especially traditionally working-class ones, UK-wide, as detailed by Wagstaff and Maynard's (1988) report on drug consumption and policy. The west coast of Scotland, with its disproportionately working-class population, would be significantly affected by this.

By 2010, professional criminals in Scotland had almost entirely halted predatory criminal activity and switched to drug-based organised crime. This transition reflected converging variables operating at transnational, national and regional levels. In collaboration with Police Scotland (Scotland's merged national force founded in 2013), the devolved Scottish Government published its plan for addressing the problem: *Scotland's Serious Organised Crime Strategy*. The report indicated that by 2015 drug supply accounted for over 70% of the countries professional crime directly and around 20% indirectly (Scottish government, 2015, p. 6). Drug supply had come to dominate the landscape of Scotland's criminal underworld. Since then, annual updates continue to indicate the most sophisticated and dangerous criminal groups to be involved, almost exclusively, in drug supply and, as a consequence, the procurement, and use, of firearms as a source of conflict resolution. This book's purpose therefore is to provide an overview and insight into the contemporary historical shift in which professional criminals in Scotland moved towards operating disproportionately in drug-based organised crime. The book identifies the break with traditional forms of professional crime and signifies those points of change in behaviour towards the unified professionalisation of organised criminal gangs dealing exclusively in drug-based crime.

In Scotland, like much of the United Kingdom, organised crime has come to predominantly express itself through the supply and distribution of drugs. Therefore, the book concentrates mainly on drug markets. While Edinburgh is Scotland's capital, Glasgow is in many ways its heart. As late as the 1980s, the city's metropolis homed over half of the country's population; as such, it is the ideal location for historical criminology research. It is here that Scotland's sectarian division frequently spilled over, that the infamous razor gangs emerged and that the nation's higher echelons of organised criminality tend to operate from. Thus, this contemporary history of drug-related organised crime in Scotland begins in Glasgow. While drug supply has gone on in various forms and guises since the late 19th century, it was only since the heroin boom in the 1980s that supply and consumption became widespread and consequently spilled over into a highly publicised 'war'. This war centred on the control and monopolisation of a blossoming drugs market. For this reason, the book focuses on the contemporary history only, but please note this term 'contemporary' is used loosely but relates to a time frame covering the past half century or so. This is why the book opened with an infamous incident which brought considerable public attention and demand for police and political intervention to tackle the growing issue of organised criminality involved in drug supply.

METHODOLOGY

In seeking to trace the shift in criminal enterprise in Scotland moving from traditional types of professional crime, such as racketeering and robbery, to criminality rooted in market processes, i.e. the illegal drugs trade, the book utilised both primary and secondary sources of data. The data for this research are largely derived from multiple sources. The bulk of the dataset used for this book originates from four independent research projects which were carried out by Robert McLean between 2012 and 2023. Thus, it is important to shed some light on the background of such research given it spans over a decade and has resulted in over 50 book, report and journal publications on the topic.

The first research project comprised data gathered from ethnographic fieldwork conducted between 2012 and 2017 as part of the Robert's PhD researching group organisation and criminal trajectories (McLean, 2018, 2019a, 2019b, 2019c). The second dataset derives from collaborative research conducted between 2017 and 2019 (McLean et al., 2019). Both studies were approved by the authors' home institution: University of the West of Scotland. The third dataset was carried out as part of group research looking at the changing landscape of youth offending in Scotland (Deuchar et al., 2021). This was conducted between 2020 and 2022. Much of the fieldwork was conducted on Glasgow's Southside and in neighbouring towns, villages and suburbs, including but by no means limited to, Barrhead, Busby, Clarkston, Giffnock, Johnstone, Linwood, Paisley, Renfrew and Thornliebank. These areas form a continuous urban expanse with the city of Glasgow. However, the second study also sought to widen the geographical scope and included fieldwork in Inverclyde, and West and South Ayrshire, as well as some limited, yet fruitful interviews from participants across the Central Belt, in the city of Edinburgh, the Highlands, and Stornoway on the Isle of Lewis. Such participants tended to be accessed through gatekeepers from the original sample in the West Coast.

Participant criteria for the first project was set as: (a) having participated in group offending, (b) having engaged in criminal behaviour defined by Police Scotland as organised crime (Scottish Government, 2015) and (c) being over 16 years of age. Participants were initially accessed via faith-based organisations, whereby outreach workers and community volunteers acted as gatekeepers. A combined purposive and snowball sampling strategy yielded 40 interviewees, primarily indigenous Caucasian males, aged from 14 to their mid-40s. Qualitative interviews typically lasted anywhere from 30 minutes to 1 hour and were one-on-one (except for two group interviews). All interviews were audio recorded, selectively transcribed and analysed thematically. The second dataset comes from a follow-up study carried out between 2017 and 2019.

A number of promising leads remained from the first study as potential interviewees had been excluded from participating owing to time constraints or the original research inclusion criteria. Therefore, this prompted a second study to be initiated free from the pressure of PhD deadlines and with more inclusive entry criteria. Participants had to (a) be, or have experience of being, involved in what Police Scotland identify as serious and organised criminal activity or (b) be involved in agencies seeking to reduce organised crime harms or (c) have been significantly affected by organised crime. In addition to outstanding leads, several charitable organisations working with (ex) offenders seeking to disengage from gangs and desist from crime were also contacted. A similar combined approach of purposive and snowball sampling yielded a second sample of 43 interviewees aged 14–60 years. 30 interviewees were offenders, eight of whom were female. All bar three male participants identified as Scottish, although not all were White or Caucasian. Participants were typically interviewed in small groups of between two and five. Five practitioners with intimate knowledge of the local drugs scene and eight local residents (seven males and one female) with histories of is shaped by the voices of actors 'situated' within Scotland's illegal drugs market, not those who seek to influence the market externally, such as law enforcement (McLean, 2019a, 2019b, 2019c).

The third dataset which contributes to data within this thesis was from independent research conducted from 2020 to 2022. Approval was granted by the University West of Scotland. The research sought to explore the changing landscape of youth and gang violence in Scotland. Both group and individual interviews were conducted in face-to-face settings and then later in an online context in accordance with the COVID-19 pandemic regulations. This produced an overall sample size of 75 participants. Interviews were conducted with 36 practitioners, including police officers, No Knives Better Lives voluntary workers, social workers and youth workers with 'Youth Point Arbourlour' and Scotland's Violence Reduction Team. In addition, 39 (ex) offenders were interviewed. The term offender here applies to any individual who has had formal systems contact due to antisocial, delinquent and/or criminal behaviour. A workable definition was applied in this respect, to account for the fact that this sample group also included children and young people ranging from 13 to 20 years of age.

In addition, as part of the current book, ethical approval was also granted by Strathclyde University to conduct further interviews, this time exclusively within an online setting, with individuals who had prior direct and/or indirect experience with consequences resulting from drug-based organised crime. This included a total of six interviews shaped by an oral historical framework.

Lynn Abrams (2010), in her book *Oral History Theory*, describes oral interviews as a methodological approach 'recording [the] speech of people with something interesting to say and then analysing their memories of the past'. While oral historians argue the recording of verbal history to be of significant importance, in that it not only capture physical 'facts' about events which took place, but more often than not, captures psychological facts, in that while discrepancies may emerge about the physicality of events, nonetheless such discussions are factual to the source discussing them, thus rendering them 'facts' (Peniston-Bird, 2008, p. 104).

Three of the six oral interviews carried out had been notable individuals involved in the criminal underworld during the 1990s. As such, they were well positioned to offer invaluable insights into sensitive topics and issues related to various events in Paisley between 1986 and 1999. These actors had previously been interviewed by the researcher as part of the prior research sample for the study conducted between 2017 and 2019. The other three interviewees had informal involvement or knowledge of criminal activity across Paisley and Glasgow. One in particular shared loose kinship with the Daniels crime family, and loose friendship with the Lyons crime family, in northern Glasgow. Interviews were recorded verbatim, before being paraphrased. This was carried out in accordance with the wishes of the interviewees due to the fear of persecution by law enforcement or retaliation by underworld figures. As such, all names, along with some details of notable dates and incidents, have been changed in order to retain participant anonymity. Additional sources of data were used to contextualise and clarify much of the oral testimony.

In accordance with practices outlined by Strathclyde University, a range of archival sources were used to provide wider background to the research topic. This included accessing several corresponding prison letters and an affidavit from key actors operating at the higher echelons of drug-based organised crime in Scotland. Letters were obtained via third-party agents. These contained insightful information written first-hand by those involved in the distribution of drugs into South Glasgow and Renfrewshire communities during the 1990s. In addition, a single partially completed diary (in several volumes) was also obtained and accessed, again via a third-party agent. The diaries contained insightful information on several events centring on the illegal supply of drugs in the Glasgow conurbation in the early 2000s. The diaries belonged to an indirect actor involved in an ongoing drug-related dispute between two notable crime families. Other sources of data were accessed via media content analysis, and the searching of key databases for public records, such as National Records Scotland, and Scottish Courts and Tribunals, as well as published reports and statistical information from HM (UK) Government, the Scottish Government, NGO reports, the UK Home Office and Police websites/webpages. Other information was obtained via a review of academic and scholarly journals, including the *Scottish Law Journal*, in an effort to gather coverage of key cases.

Researching organised crime is difficult, and direct observations can of course be risky, while infiltration of willing participants involved in such activities can also be complicated – practically as well as ethically (Windle, 2013). Autobiographies use an insider's voice and can prove an important tool for gathering what would otherwise be inaccessible information. This is particularly true when autobiographies are patchworked with other data sources in order to plug gaps in knowledge. Despite being utilised in a number of studies on organised crime (Hobbs, 2013) and terrorism (Shapiro & Siegel, 2012), Morselli (2003) argues autobiographies are nonetheless all too often overlooked and thus remain an underused source. Indeed, Ken Plummer (2001) argues that autobiographies should not be seen strictly as objective accounts, but when used as sources of supplementary information, they can prove invaluable. Using such a methodology to recount the events of 'the Essex Boys' murders, Criminologist James Windle (2013) stresses the need to 'investigate' and 'validate' accounts utilising alternative sources.

Autobiographies were used here both to fill knowledge gaps and validate participant accounts. This method proved useful when coupled with insider knowledge of recorded events. This included autobiographies of gangland enforcer, turned publisher, Paul Ferris, often co-authored by the late Reg McKay. The author(s) compiled four books in total: *Ferris Conspiracies* (Ferris & McKay, 2001), *Vendetta* (Ferris, 2005), *Villains* (Ferris & McKay, 2010) and *Deadly Divisions* (Ferris & McKay, 2002). Additional McKay autobiographies which were also used, although to a lesser extent, included *The Last Godfather* (McKay, 2007), *McGrew* (McKay, 2010), *Murder Capital* (McKay, 2006) and *Armed Candy* (McKay, 2002). *Armed Candy* in particular was written using a series of pseudonyms and thus could only be deciphered with insider accounts to compare and check against. It was useful as it discussed the activities of the now-deceased Stuart Boyd, who played a pivotal role in the criminal underworld in the late 1980s and 1990s. In addition to McKay's publications, former investigative journalist and organised crime fighter, Russell Findlay MSP's publications *The Iceman*, *Caught in the Crossfire* and *Acid Attack* are also used (Findlay, 2008, 2012, 2018, respectively). The latter book was written and published as a result of a coordinated acid attack on Findlay by those involved in organised crime for published investigative pieces on their activities. While there remain a number of questions regarding validity surrounding the use of autobiographical information, the publications proved informative when combined with methods of triangulation to offer insight into key events, instances and the role of actors. Indeed, while details are often vague, distorted or overlooked, they do provide an overarching sense of ensuing narratives around triangulated data.

CHAPTER SYNOPSIS

This chapter introduced the contemporary history of organised drug crime in Scotland as the book's focus. This has been achieved by setting the background to the topic, indicating a change in criminal behaviour from predatory crime or crime against people towards market-based crime: namely the illicit drugs trade. The introductory chapter likewise set out the research question, justified the study and set boundaries, scope and focus. The remainder of the chapter provides a chapter synopsis, followed by a chapter summary. The chapter synopsis overviews the book. The second chapter of the book is the literature review, centred on the topic of organised crime. While early research on organised crime looks primarily at predatory-based crimes, over time organised crime has become ever more intertwined with drug supply. These two areas of research have been brought increasingly closer since 2000, reflecting the growth of Britain's illicit drug markets. The first part of chapter two traces the origins, and coinage, of the term organised crime, and notes how what was essentially a US phenomenon became extrapolated into the European and British arenas. The chapter then moves to discuss how professional criminality and gang formation in the European and British contexts gradually became intertwined with drug supply.

Chapter 3 provides a background to contextualise the study. It is important to understand the context broadly speaking given that social, economic, political and cultural factors inevitably shape how phenomena is perceived, understood and unfolds. Given that the research is focused on the Scottish dimension of drug-based organised crime, and that the west coast of the country has consistently been highlighted as having disproportionate levels of violence, gangs, drug harms and organised criminal activity, the chapter provides some background on the development of the largest urban settlement in the region: the Glasgow conurbation. In discussing the Glasgow conurbation, the chapter illustrates how particular periods of time, and certain contextual settings, impacted upon the type of crime, gangs and criminals that emerged. Looking at the formation and subsequent industrialisation of Glasgow, the thesis again draws attention to the infamous razor gangs of the 1920s and 1930s, as identified by historian Andrew Davies in his book *City of Gangs* (2013). These sectarian gangs were a product of the socio-economic and cultural factors of the time but have had a lasting impact on the city by installing a deeply embedded knife culture. This discussion allows the book's attention to turn to the gangs of the post-war era, and examination of the 'glocalised' shift towards the emergence of market-based organised crime. The chapter discusses how the new urban landscape, located in a globalised context, allows for certain practices, industries and employment to become intertwined with market-based organised crime. This in turn allows drugs to become the central feature of organised crime in the United Kingdom, following developments in the heroin market in the 1980s.

Chapters 4 and 5 continue to look directly at the development of market-based organised crime in the form of the illicit drug trade throughout the 1990s. Given the impact on organised crime in Scotland, the chapter focuses extensively on the unofficially coined 'Paisley Drugs War' (PDW) in detail and looks to discuss how the shift from predatory-based to market-based organised crime centred on the growth of the drugs trade, most notably the supply of heroin and prescribed opioids such as Temazepam. The PDW marked a significant shift as criminals on a wider scale, brought up during the 1980s heroin boom, now sought to capitalise on the drugs they once consumed as adolescents. The PDW would, as is seen, result in over a dozen deaths over a decade, as well as stabbings, shootings and political corruption.

Chapter 6 proceeds to appraise the second drugs war in Scotland. The chapter focuses on a series of events which has unofficially been coined the Daniels v Lyons drug war. The early 2000s saw the PDW decline as key actors became incarcerated or were murdered as a result of fighting between and within gangs. The conflict left a void which disrupted learning between generations of gang members. The Daniels–Lyons drug war has essentially shaped Scotland's modern landscape in regard to drug-based organised crime. The chapter focuses on the beginning of the feud, stimulated itself by the growth of the drug trade, and how both family-based criminal groups would adopt different tactics to overcome obstacles. The chapter likewise discusses how changes in law enforcement usage of the term organised crime impacted on how such criminal activities and actors were perceived and projected in political and public realms, including media coverage.

Chapter 7 is essentially divided into two distinct parts. The first part considers the contemporary setting Scotland finds itself in, in relation to organised crime. The second part entails a concluding discussion. The chapter thus opens by building upon the prior chapters to analyse how the contemporary drugs market has evolved in such a way that organised criminal gangs have largely ceased efforts to monopolise activity, either through controlling product or actors, and instead now operate as mutual competitors based on product quality, availability and purity. The chapter explores alterative distribution methods, and how global processes, in the economic, political and cultural realms, significantly affect the local environment. The chapter discusses the case of notable actors involved in international drug smuggler, such as 'The Gillespie Brothers'. The activity of the Gillespie Brothers in many ways mimics that of other organised criminal groups across the international arena, such as Sicilian and American Mafiosi, as well as the Mexican and South American cartels. A comparative analysis explores some of the given similarities and differences. The chapter then considers the impact transitional criminal networks, and technological advances, have upon local environment and criminal behaviour in terms of bring in different drug types, actors and supply methods, which differ from traditional forms. The second part, i.e. the concluding discussion, draws upon findings and seeks to situate and understand the development of drug-based organised crime within the wider national and international arena, providing a comparative analysis with other contextual settings. The discussion is likewise linked to wider literature covered on the subject. The chapter highlights research limitations, before, thereafter, providing recommendations to practice and policy in order to allow for a better understanding, and tackling, of organised crime in Scotland.

CHAPTER SUMMARY

This introductory chapter's purpose was to acquaint the reader with the research topic, sources and methods and the book in overview. The book provides an overview of the development of organised crime in Scotland, shedding light on those multi-complexities which converged to result in traditional professional criminals involved primarily in predatory-based organised crime against people, to transition to concentrate almost exclusively on drug-based organised crime. As such, the book ultimately seeks to trace the contemporary history of drug-based organised crime in Scotland. The methodological discussion also draws attention to some of the challenges and difficulties oral historians may face when conducting research located within sensitive subject areas: in this case organised criminality, and details how the researchers sought to overcome such difficulties in validating accounts. The chapter then provided a chapter synopsis for the book. Chapter 2 reviews literature relating to the phenomenon of organised crime.

2

PINNING DOWN ORGANISED CRIME: LITERATURE REVIEW

CHAPTER INTRODUCTION

Having broadly introduced Scottish organised crime's move into the illicit drugs trade, this chapter contextualises the topic in extant literature. The literature covered here focuses on the topic of organised crime, broadly speaking, given its application as an umbrella concept capturing a variety of criminal activity, and discussions concerning drug-based crime. This covers such criminal activity's origins, definition and structure among other aspects. This chapter begins by looking explicitly at the origins of the terms itself, before moving towards a wider discussion of how such practice manifests itself within the international arena. The review proceeds to focus on practice within the United Kingdom, and how the term organised crime has in many ways become synonymous with drug-based criminal activity within contemporary Britain. Thereafter, the literature review will briefly discuss illegal drug markets in the United Kingdom in order to shed light on the extent of the problem and the way in which distribution occurs. A summary concludes this chapter.

ORIGINS OF ORGANISED CRIME TERMINOLOGY

Terminology and perception are intertwined. The term organised crime tends to conjure images of early 1920s gangsters in the United States, such as Chicago's Al Capone or New York City's Charles 'Lucky' Luciano. Characters like Capone and Luciano are often perceived as holding a contradictory dual position in society. They are respected and revered in legitimate society because of wealth, power and prestige, yet this power is derived from a base of fear and intimidation acquired through underworld criminal activity. Much of the perception and stereotypes surrounding these gangsters however is more fiction than fact. Indeed, this is true of organised crime more generally. Conceptualisations of organised crime, as used today, are essentially an invention of US politics, media and law enforcement. While origins of the term itself can be traced back to at least the early 19th century, it was not until the early 20th century that the term became consistent in application of meaning (Von Lampe, 2016). Since then, although inspired by debates on organised crime in the United States, the term has in many respects come to be adopted widely by other countries. Typically, this involved a process involving US think tanks pushing political and at times economic agendas also (See Gootenburg, 2012). This is particularly true in Europe where the term has been used, sporadically at first, in the post-war era and then more frequently from the 1990s onwards. Indeed, during the run up to, and in the immediate aftermaths of, the UN Convention against Transnational Organised Crime, aka and hereafter the Palermo Convention, in 2000, the term has been adopted on a global scale. Organised crime in many ways exemplifies how problems within modern societies are identified and then placed on the political agenda of global society (Densley et al., 2018).

The combination of the two words *organised* and *crime* first appeared intermittently, and then with increased frequency, in the English language in media sources and official government reports from approximately the 1830s onwards in both America and Britain. According to Von Lampe's (2016) comprehensive review of the development of organised crime as a concept and practice, while the meaning of such combination fluctuated, it can essentially be placed into two main contextual clusters between 1800 and 1920. The first cluster is used in reference to the political realm. Here, early combination of the term tended to refer to crimes committed in wartime. This included atrocities committed by military personal in the 1860–65 US Civil War regarding acts within the defeated Confederate States or those committed by the British Empire during its colonial ventures: perhaps most notably in India between 1858 and 1947. However, the term was also used occasionally as a method for denouncing labour union movements. Von Lampe however emphasises the need to apply some degree of caution regarding its application of meaning given that the term *organised* was a popular prefix between the mid-nineteenth and early twentieth centuries, often associated with processes of modernisation. In *Modernity and the Holocaust*, Zigmunt Bauman (1989) suggests the terminology is used to reflect the epitome of social engineering within a structural socialist paradigm proved popular in this period discussed.

The second cluster refrains from political application and instead contains references used to describe more conventional types of crimes that tend to have some degree of planned execution. Concerning conventional crimes, the term organised crime was more popularly applied to those crimes that mimicked opportunistic and predatory behaviours, such as theft and robbery: as opposed to market-based crimes, which involved various logistical processes and independently operant agencies. Pioneering Chicago school theorist Edwin Sutherland's *The Professional Thief* (1937) offers an ethnographic account of such conventional types of crime, whereby the working professional criminal pickpockets, robs and cons unsuspecting civilians, even targeting wealthy and powerful people to maximise profits. During this period, the term organised crime would be used to refer to criminal activities in this generic sense.

At the heart of the second cluster reference to organised and planned criminality is the murder of New Orleans police Chief David Hennessey, by two Italian immigrant men with ties to a traditionally foreign, Sicilian, organisation coined the 'mafia', in 1890 (Kennedy, 2018). The public murder of Hennessey caused considerable outrage among the public and fuelled a growing moral panic over a steady influx of southern European immigrants. *The New York Times* even raised the question for public debate as to whether almost half a million Italian immigrants had imported themselves into US society, bringing with them characteristic methods of banding themselves into secret, oath-bound networks bent on crime. *Harpers Weekly* also supported the view that oath-bound, murderous societies were being propagated by Sicilian immigrants into the United States. In retaliation, hysteria would see southern vigilante groups of US citizens attack and kill a number of Italian immigrants. Further fuelling the situation were a growing number of kidnappings by a criminal organisation known as The Black Hand, due to its calling card.

Yet, Von Lampe notes the significant impact of the deliberate usage of the term in the 1919 Chicago Crime Commission report. The impact of the report cannot be underestimated as it consolidated the notion of the professional criminal as a perpetual threat to legitimate society in the minds of the business and entrepreneurial class. As noted, this is perhaps due to the composition of the Commission itself. The Commission was a civic organisation set up by and for prominent businessmen, bankers, lawyers and other white-collar professionals, concerned at the time with the perceived notion that organised crime, primarily in the form of predatory criminal activity, was systematic in nature and as such could cause significant harm to business, and even to the wider economic growth of cities like Chicago. In the pronouncements of the Chicago Crime Commission, organised crime would be a term used to refer not to criminal organisations *pe se* but one applied in wider reference to the existence of a criminal class network. This used criminal contacts and exploited corrupt business practices to profit from illegal activity (Sims, 1920). Yet the events that would unfold during the forthcoming US Probation era (1920–1933) embedded this notion of organised crime as occurring within a criminal class but brought racist connotations with it.

The Prohibition Era is perhaps unhelpfully perceived to be the result of indigenous protestant moral entrepreneurs advocating for the outlaw of the production and sale of alcohol (Reinarman, 1979). In reality, prohibition was the result of much more numerous, combining factors, converging in a perfect storm: ranging from the increased political pressure from temperance movements, to changing industrialist attitudes, and feelings of resentment towards newly arriving global south immigrants (Von Lampe, 2016). Whatever the reasons for Prohibition, this period undoubtedly proved significant in shaping perception as to how organised crime would be understood and perceived by future law enforcement and the political establishment. Prohibition was widely unpopular itself; thus, supply and demands processes created ideal conditions for previously legal activities, i.e. the procurement, sale and consumption of alcohol, to move into the realm of the illegal economy. Initially, those in positions of power in the public sphere, such as politicians and business owners, would utilise affiliations with individuals and groups who had connections to the criminal underworld in order to enable the production and sale of alcohol to continue. Specialised federal police units were created in response to the pressure to crack down on alcohol's sale and consumption. This process only served to heighten existing tensions and escalate related violence. By the late 1920s, organised crime was no longer associated with an amorphous 'criminal class', but rather to 'gangsters', 'gangs' and 'syndicates' (McLean, 2019a). It was no longer seen as a product of conditions that could be remedied by means of social and political reform but rather had to be tackled by rigorous law enforcement, as stated in *The New York Times* spread titled *War on Organized Crime* (New York Times, 1993, p. 1). While various criminals were involved in supplying illegal alcohol during prohibition, a few prominent figures captured the imagination at the time. This included the notable Al Capone, among others with Italian heritage. Drawing upon already existing stereotypes, the public association of organised crime with Italian immigrants and secret criminal organisations would only be heightened. Yet, such stereotypes would become firmly cemented in the preceding years, with televised hearings investigating organised criminality.

By the 1950s, a number of American media reports, coinciding with nationally televised hearings held by the US Senate committee, then chaired by

Estes Kefauver, would result in a resurgence of public imagery associated with Italian mafia groups. This process would also bring a convergence of the two clusters or categorisations of organised crime terminology as noted by Von Lampe above: where political and conventional elements of crime would become intertwined. The Committee was set up to tackle increased criminality in illegal racketeering and illegal gambling. Following proceedings, the committee concluded that numerous criminal groups throughout the United States were tied together by 'a sinister criminal organisation known as Mafia' (Senate Rep. 1951, p. 2). The work of FBI agent and criminologist Donald Cressey was influential in the conceptual development of Mafia blueprints. The FBI would conclude most organised crime in the United States to be headed by, or intertwined with, *Mafiosi* leadership to some degree. Some analysts, however, note that perhaps, rather than revealing a true understanding of Mafia, Cressey and colleagues, unable in their ideological thinking to accurately dissect, or even begin to understand, complex cultural relationships spanning both intergenerational and transnational communities, could only understand such phenomenon through their own habitual lens, and thus conceptualised Mafia in their own FBI image. However, as a result, the US Congress would eventually seek to tackle organised crime head on by outlawing Mafia – or *Cosa Nostra* – associations. This was achieved by the passing of the 1970 Racketeer Influenced and Corrupt Organizations (RICO) Act. This meant that even loose association with known felons could result in arrest (Kefauver, 1951). In preceding years, numerous state level commissions and specialised law enforcement units were set up to tackle organised crime. Critically though it is important to note that competitive allocation of police funds was often dependent upon the existence of state-run organised crime syndicates. Since then, however, US-led debates within the international realm have consistently extrapolated the term to other parts of the world.

Having traced the historical development and application associated imagery of organised crime as a term, the analysis turns to relevant literature discussing organisational structures and activity for those who engage in it in practice. This is primarily applied to the international, then the United Kingdom, contexts. However, in drawing out relevant literature, it is important to first set out definition as applied in this specific research. The European Union (EU) adheres to the UNODC (2021) protocols, in derived from the Palermo Convention. Thus, it recognises that organised crime involves more than one person, is organised, causes significant harm and benefits those involved. Von Lampe (2016, p. 74) further identifies organised crime activity as three pronged: being (a) market-based thus pertaining to the provision of illegal goods/services, (b) predatory crimes, involving exploitation of others and (c) illegal-governance crimes, involving the illegitimate exercise of power to regulate behaviour. Furthermore, Campana and Varese (2018) operationalise the third category, *extra-legal governance*, based on three measures: the ability to generate communal fear, coerce legal businesses and influence official figures. They argue that extra-legal governance clusters in less affluent or deprived areas and neighbourhoods, characterised by a lack of trust in legitimate institutions. Accordingly, this book only applies the term organised crime to those drug markets and criminal group meeting these defining criteria (McLean, 2019a, 2019b, 2019c, p XXIV).

INTERNATIONAL ORGANISED CRIME IN PRACTICE

As historian, and mafioso expert, John Dickie notes in *Cosa Nostra: The Definitive History of the Sicilian Mafia* (2007), one can only really understand America's so-called foreign menace by understanding the history of their Southern Italian counterparts. In his work, Dickie details, in great depth, the political and economic conditions which saw their Sicilian predecessors cement this 'brotherhood' and 'oath bound culture' into Southern Italian society. Dickie points to the rural landscape of the country and feudal economic system, that allowed criminality to become embedded into the political establishment prior to capitalism. Not long after the formation of a united Italy in 1871, following Garibaldi's exploits in the post-Napoleon era, Dickie argues ongoing political unrest from the southern states, who saw themselves as culturally different from their Northern counterparts, led to mutual distrust. In addition, while the north grew democratic and economically prosperous, the south remained underfunded; its inhabitants treated as second-class citizens. This political and economic system, accompanied by an existing cultural code of hypermasculine behaviour (Rafanell et al., 2017), whereby vendettas were common, leads to independent townships banding together under common oaths of protection and cooperation. Dickie notes while the term *mafia* is used as an umbrella described here, there were in fact many organisations independently named, such as the Cosa Nostra and Camorra. Outsiders venturing into these townships would be treated with suspicion, and legitimate external business investors would be targeted for extortion and/or vandalism. Police corruption allowed mafioso to commit crimes and even embed themselves into positions of legitimate society, such as law enforcement, and political office. Dickie (2012) similarly details in *Mafia Brotherhoods: Camorra, mafia, 'Ndrangheta: the rise of the Honoured Societies* the rise and inevitable perpetuation, of these independent organisations, as honour and social status based on toxic notions of manhood, demanding retaliation against any perceived slight.

From the mid-19th century to the early 20th century, the number of Italian immigrants in the United States reached approximately four million. This coincided with the growth of the city of Chicago. In his classic 1927 study *The Gang*, Frederic Thrasher deemed the city to be an ethnic melting pot, in which the socio-economic conditions created a criminogenic breeding ground. While the term *mafia* itself was rarely used in media outlets when referencing 'public enemy' Al Capone and his bootlegging criminal syndicate, contemporary cinematic hindsight recreates mafia imagery. Both Woodiwiss and Lombardo point out corruption, in the form of an established political structure impeding law enforcement enabled Chicago to become 'the most corrupt city in the US in the early 1900s'. Concurring with the work of Dickie, Lombardo (2013) likewise states extrapolated Sicilian culture regarded police enforcement of business as 'alien' and to be challenged (p. 298). While other American professional criminals concentrated on predatory crimes, Italian Americans continued in developing market-based criminality, aimed at perpetuating financial income streams. While using political power to tap into the Trade Unions, the Italian American Mafia would enter the booming post-war casino industry, to skim profits, and launder money through real estate investment. Albanese notes an increase in organised crime tends to correlate with an increased murder rate (2014, p. 13).

In *The Vory* (2018), Mark Galeotti offers a historical analysis of the development of organised crime from pre-war Tsarist Russia to the Putin era. Similarly to Dickie's account of Cosa Nostra, Galeotti argues political instability, combined with a vastly rural and feudal economic system, contributed to the lack of state ability to enforce centralised power across the nation. This allowed criminal practice to embed itself into the political establishment, accumulating oligarchical power among a now 'criminal elite'. Following the end of the Cold War, Russia would increase trade with the western world. Consequently, the black market flourished as Soviet-made weaponry moved outwards and into conflict zones, militia stockpiles and the global criminal fraternity. Meanwhile, western money, technology and goods moved East. Dutch historian Stephen Snelders (2021) likewise argues former colonial and post-industrial countries, like the Netherlands, benefit from pre-existing infrastructure, allowing rapid supply of goods whenever opportunistic demands are created, within both legal and illegal markets. Snelders draws attention to existing colonial trade routes enabling Dutch entrepreneurs to form rapid partnerships to engage in distribution and supply: for example, the supply of amphetamines and Ecstasy/MDMA to the United Kingdom. As such, it is important to note, many criminal networks like those highlighted by Snelders bear little resemblance to imagery of mafia syndicates.

Organised crime in such context can differ between countries, even displaying regional differences within them. Rege (2016) studied organised crime in India and found that the countries 'Sand Mafia', bore little resemblance to their Italian counterparts. Rather, their name comes from illegally mining sand for the construction industry: an operation which involves a multitude of fragmented structures supported by transient memberships. Given India has the third largest construction market, after China and America, demand for sand outstrips its legal availability (Rege, 2016, p. 101). Its operation entails diverse interdependencies geared towards specific goals at each stage. Like the Indian Sand Mafia, in Japan, the Yakuza display unique characteristics, often intertwined with the legitimate economy, financial and corporate industry and political structures. The organisation cherishes association with its traditional fiefdoms and seeks not to impede their reach into other continents, barring a brief spell in San Francisco in the United States over the 1980s. The latter exception resulted during the growth of Japan's 'Bubble Economy' where the Yakuza harvested billions of US dollars. At the time, commentators remarked the Yakuza to be a 'massive hedge fund' with billions held in investible assets cloaked by its quasi-legitimate status (Kaplan & Dubro, 2012, p. 11). However, in an era of increased transnational trade, the Yakuza have formed close ties with Russian mafia and bankrolled rackets in China.

Indeed, Broadhurst and Wa (2009) note that organised crime has flourished in both Hong Kong and the Chinese mainland since the end of the Cold War. The southern China-originating Triads are an active organised crime syndicate, whose business includes, akin to the US-based Italian mafia, protection services to economic actors working in mainly easy-to-access markets of legal and illegal commodities. Triads existed among the original inhabitants of Hong Kong prior to 1842 when the British Empire cited it and lean towards historical associational ties with rebels and avengers as well as the monks of the Shaolin Temple. Within China and Honk Kong, the Triads are considered a significant threat to legitimate enterprise and partake in opportunistic ventures, such as drug trafficking, gambling, prostitution, debt collecting, human smuggling and loan sharking.

Given the needs of secrecy and resources, a number of contemporary scholars note significant overlap between organised criminal groups and terrorists (for instance Shelley & Picarelli, 2005). Indeed, differences can be subtle and difficult to distinguish. Drawing on means utilised in the case of the 2004 Madrid train bombing, Picarelli (2012) notes how criminal networks overlap and feed into one another, stating 'organized crime and terrorism are both an organization and an activity…[both] forms of social activity and the organizations that conduct those activities' (p. 182). For example, in Latin America, symbiotic ties are witnessed in Brazil, Argentina and Paraguay where organised crime and terrorist groups overlap with shared cultural affinities, using resources from one another, accessing the same trade routes and partners and sharing membership. Following the Yugoslavian Wars, a number of Balkan states organised various militia groups. Organised criminal activity concerning the shipment of drugs, cigarettes and counterfeit goods into Western Europe provided income streams that would fund terrorist groups and militias fighting political causes. This was so even in Columbia, where Pablo Escobar headed one of several notable cartels supplying drugs, namely cocaine, into the United States. Yet these funds would be used to assist Escobar engage in terrorist activities against the state, in order to maintain power (Smolíková & Smolík, 2011).

Gootenberg (2012) draws attention to the difficulty the US government has in stemming the flow of illegal narcotics flowing across US borders, overseen by Mexican Cartels. Gootenberg points out prior trade laws between North American states have in many ways monopolised the proceeds of legitimate capitalism in favour of the United States. As a result, Mexico's biggest export is drugs, which is three times the value of the second largest export, oil. This imbalance only serves to fuel criminality, as political parties advocate for change in the public domain but take bribes and accepts degrees of corruption in secret. Thus, it is impossible to separate the illegitimate activities of powerful Cartels from the legitimate state, as long as structural economic imbalance remains.

Organised Crime in Britain

Following the Palermo Convention in 2000, the United Kingdom sought to enact and implement new legislation against organised crime. As noted in the introductory chapter, formerly those engaged in crime for financial profit as a means to earning a livelihood and/or engaging in particular lifestyles consistently would typically be deemed professional criminals. This is supported by the work of leading organised crime scholars Dick Hobbs and Georgios Antonopoulos (2013a, 2013b), who drew extensively upon twentieth-century police and media records to illustrate the lack of organised crime terminology in the United Kingdom prior to 2000. They instead draw attention to the use of terms like 'professional criminal' to distinguish those who commit crime as a means to ongoing financial gain and those who are simply convicted of a crime. New legislation however demanded organised crime terminology be adopted and the phenomena acknowledged in its fullest. As such, the UK government and law enforcement commissioned multiple research projects publications recognising the threat and extent of organised crime. Dedicated specialised police units would be established, including the National Crime Agency and Police Scotland's own version, which has undergone several name changes but is currently known as Scotland Serious Organised Crime Taskforce (SOCT). In recognising overlaps between terrorism, the higher echelons of organised crime and serious harms caused at the lower end, UK law enforcement incorporates the prefix term *serious* to allow workability in practice and avoid potentially counterproductive rigid definitions being transferred into law.

Reports by Kirby and Nailor (2013) estimated the United Kingdom 'to have 38,000 offenders operating within 6,000 organized crime groups' (p. 398). The UK's Serious Organised Crime Assessment (SOCA) 2006–2007 commented that organized crime is guided by: '[...] profit, risk, opportunity and capability. [Most] serious organized criminal activity is directly or indirectly concerned with making money' (p. 52). Furthermore, SOCA argued collaboration is essential for the formation of organised crime groups. Different criminal activities require different organisational structures; the tight knit design, for example, operates for armed robberies. Established criminal groups are typically involved in at least two profit-making criminal activities, often, drug trafficking and money laundering. Aside from the United Kingdom's official policing perspectives, academic studies identify the presence in the United Kingdom of several forms of organised crime that do not always fit the envelope of SOCA. The landscape of criminological investigation is varied in its focus. While it is legitimate to emphasise national jurisdiction that emphasis can distort if it denies connections with wider networks that are transnational (Segel, 2010). Most academic research in Britain focuses on organised crime structure, activity and definition in a generic sense. Most case studies looking at the criminal activities of particular groups and individuals tend to take the form of autobiographies. Many of these will be looked at more specifically in forthcoming chapters and thus will not be included here. As Hobbs and Antonopoulos (2013a, 2013b) note, most UK-focused research on organised crime tends to take the form of either former paramilitary organisations now engaged in economic criminality, the old professional criminals such as Ronny Briggs or traditional crime families centred on kinship.

The 1998 Good Friday Agreement effectively ended the ethno-nationalist conflict termed 'The Troubles' in Northern Ireland. As such, former paramilitary networks remained intact yet obsolete. Perhaps inevitably, a number of these groups would use existing resources to move into organised criminality for economic pursuit. This tended to revolve around firearm and drug trafficking. Notable organised crime expert and commenter Dick Hobbs' (2013) ethnographies of organised crime offer a frame through which to better understand the cultural setting of the organised crime-terrorist enterprises in Northern Ireland. Hobb's explains 'specific political and economic environments produced cultural interpretations that located market relations as a central driver of everyday life' (p. 2). According to Hobbes, a professional criminal culture enables social ties in such an environment and is a characteristic of British-organised crime during the current and past centuries. Illegal trading is associated with a 'good life' by young criminals and worthy of pursuit for those who carry the various forms of capital required, against a backdrop of economic and political restrictions. In the context of London's criminal culture, Hobbs depicts organised crime as a countercultural to the capital's perceived hedonistic values.

Sergi (2015) extends the work of Hobbs into the British mainland and identifies organised crime being a group of unlawful activities committed by criminals working together, not single individuals dominating an underworld. Sergi relates that since the 1990s, professional criminals incorporated into their *modus operandi* an entrepreneurial trading culture exploiting global markets, and, concurring with Snelders, utilised existing infrastructure from colonial and industrial pasts to do so. England has a tradition of organised criminal groups being regarded as local gang-style interfaces pursuing economic, as opposed to political, crime (Crocker et al., 2019). Crocker et al. draw attention to the socio-economic domain in which organised crime takes hold in Britain. Crocker and colleagues aver that UK-organised crime tends to be 'local [and] driven...by the physical and social environment of the neighbourhood in which [it] resides' (2019, p. 434). Criminal groups are nested within and concealed by communities, whose norms they work alongside, primarily dealing in demand processes such as drug supply. Structures tend to be family-based and include horizontal and hierarchic drivers of decision-making and command. Their sociality played out mainly within their housing schemes where status was projected through the ownership of material goods, such as prestigious cars, branded clothing and wristwatches.

Most research on British organised crime comes from official police and governmental sources. Academic research tends to incorporate qualitative date from interviewees, yet, as noted in this book's introduction, first-hand accounts are typically given through autobiographies. Indeed, public imagery of organised crime in Britain tends to be formed through dramatised media portrayals and includes loosely based versions of stories attributed to the Kray Twins, Paul Ferris and the Essex Boys. Scholar James Windle (2013) however draws upon several autobiographical accounts to detail the criminal career of the Essex boys. Typically, this includes the work of former Essex Boys associate, turned crime writer, Bernard O'Malley. Windle's accounts support official and academic research that criminal groups tend to operate locally and within communities that share some degree of cultural conceptualisations of behaviour and masculinity. Crimes tended to revolve around drug supply. The Essex boys in many ways typified organised crime groups of the 1990s and early 2000s. Forces of demand, restriction of opportunity and hedonistic ideals drove criminal behaviour. The Essex Boys were infamously gunned down in 1995.

Other historical and autobiographical accounts of British-organised crime tend to centre on the trafficking of drugs or other drug-related activities. A range of publications include *Cocky*, by Tony Barnes et al. (2011), who recalls the account of Curtis Warren from Merseyside, considered to be the United Kingdom's most profitable drug trafficker with transnational connections. Curtis would use his connection to the security trade to supply (night) clubbers with drugs. Later, Curtis would oversee the international trafficking of drug supply routes from the Netherlands to form connections with other criminals UK-wide. Other books focus on the other related aspect of drug distribution, such as protection. Graham Johnson's 2007 book *The Devil: Britain's Most Feared Underworld Taxman* provides an account of martial arts expert Stephen French who terrorised the new criminal class of upcoming entrepreneurial drug dealing in post-industrial Liverpool. Johnson recalls, in the words of French, how old-style professional criminals, who formerly engaged in heist and bank robbery, either moved into drug dealing as demand for drugs like cannabis, ecstasy and heroin grew during the late 1970s–1990s or acted as 'taxmen' demanding protection payment from primarily those upcoming criminals distributing drugs. These distributors perhaps lacked the criminal clout to avoid becoming targets for traditional 'hardmen'.

More recently, and specifically regarding the Scottish context, McLean and colleagues published a number of works detailing the growth of organised crime in the country between 2015 and 2023 (Densley et al., 2018, 2019; Deuchar et al., 2020; Harding et al., 2019; Holligan et al., 2019, 2020; McLean et al., 2019a, 2019b). Prior to 2010, much public and political attention was given to the problem of territorial youth gangs engaged in knife-related violence. However, coinciding with the decline of these recreational street gangs was the sharp increase in organised criminality related to drug-based crime. The above-noted scholars relate the manner in which socio-economic, cultural and political factors converged to bring about a shift in gang behaviour as they evolved to mirror their English, and even to some degree US counterparts, in displaying behaviours more akin to organised drug-based criminality within the last decade. Such criminal practice is reflected in wider drug harm data and trends overall, showing that behaviour in one sphere impacts on the other.

ILLEGAL DRUGS MARKETS: DEFINING MARKETS AND CURRENCY

Having analysed the historical development of organised crime as a term and phenomenon and illumined its practice in the international and UK contexts, attention turns to the growth of the United Kingdom's illegal drug markets. This clarifies the extent and impact of drug-related organised crime. In order to address the issue, one might begin by asking, what exactly is a drugs market? The term 'market' here is a loose analogy, applied as a conceptualisation, to help explain processes involved in acquiring, moving and distributing certain products, which may also include wider services, from those who organise and purchase initial goods before selling to others involved in such sales or directly to consumers (Reynolds, 2020). Involvement is generally incentivised by financial gains, although some social, economic and political incentives may also be important. Actors operate at various levels, individually, in groups and in networks, in order to help facilitate movement of goods and services provided (McLean et al., 2017). The term market is not to be thought of as a solid tangible thing, but rather as a concept with fluid boundaries. Thus, what is a market to some may not be a market to another.

How one applies the term drug of course has significant implications as to how a 'drugs' market is defined. *In Fierce Chemistry: A History of UK Drug Wars*, Harry Shapiro (2021) offers up an excellent historical analysis of Britain's ongoing war with drug use, distribution and consumption. Shapiro argues that society generally applies a narrow view as to what constitutes a drug. Although the general perception is that drugs are illegal – or involve the misuse of legal – substances peddled in the criminal underworld, when analysing the biological process whereby substances are ingested, impacting upon the central nervous system to alter feelings, then drugs range from opium to alcohol to teas, coffees and sugars. Shapiro estimates the total global value of such a trade, taking a broad definition, can be approximated at $1.4 trillion. However, such definitions would be too broad for this book's purposes. Indeed, even Europol's European Monitoring Centre for Drugs and Drug

Addiction (EMCDDA), who regularly issue updated reports on Europe's illegal drugs markets, fail to provide clarity as to the actual definition being applied in defining drugs. Instead, the research here adopts a workable definition as an answer to the problem. When discussing illegal drug markets, generally, the term is applied to those outlawed substances acknowledged by the EMCDDA in their EU Drug Market Reports, including cannabis, heroin and opioids, cocaine, synthetic drugs and new psychoactive substances. Yet, the research acknowledges any definition will be inherently exclusive, omitting a variety of other substance types.

Having defined drugs and markets, we briefly turn to issues of currency. Recent research increasingly indicates that currency has changed in organised crime. While money remains the primary form of currency for paying for goods, a number of leading scholars in the field, such as Campana and Varese (2019), argue significant changes in organised criminal networks have seen drugs move from not only being a product for purchase but also a commodity with financial value acting as currency. African criminal groups in particular have been known to pay for goods and services through blood diamonds. South American cartels have likewise increasingly begun to use drugs themselves as currency. In a number of published works, renowned ethnographic researcher Loic Wacquant similarly (2000, 2008, 2010) points out that drugs are widely used as a form of street currency within communities he terms as *hyper-ghettos*. Thus, while overall money in the area may be low, drug currency may remain high: a process which inevitably affects community stability. Given that currency may change in drug markets, this will inevitably impact upon how market estimates are measured and perceived. For this book's purposes, therefore, drugs may in certain contexts be regarded as currency rather than merely as products.

Estimating the Scale of the Illegal Drugs Trade

Illegal drug markets and drug trafficking routes exist throughout the vast majority of countries worldwide, with the scale of cultivation, production and distribution of illicit substances continuing to grow year on year (McSweeney et al., 2008). Indeed, in 2019, the UNODC estimated approximately 275 million people worldwide aged 15–64, accounted for one in every 18 people in that age group, had used drugs at least once in the previous year. This corresponds to 5.5% of the global population aged 15–64. Between 2010 and 2019, the estimated number of past-year users of any drug globally increased by 22%. The global trade is regarded to be the largest and most lucrative business venture for organised criminals (Densley et al., 2022). Approximating the monetary value generated globally by the trade is fraught with difficulty for a number of reasons, ranging from currency to drug purity to the secretive nature of those actors who operate within. Yet the UNODC currently estimates the illegal drugs trade to be approx. $360 per annum. Giommoni et al. (2020) have traced the development and prospects of international drug markets, including the ramifications of 'darknet' communications technology in this area (see also Gundur, 2020).

After the United States, Europe is the world's second most popular destination for illegal drug supply. Efforts have been made to estimate the value of the drug market in this context. Figures collated by the EMCDDA and Europol estimate a value of EUR 30 billion annually. This is based on EU citizens' spending on illegal drugs. Although the above figures are considerably different in scale, they shed light on the size of the market at different ends of the supply chain. Estimations by UNODC (2005) and EMCDDA and Europol (2019), for example, each represent an estimation of the value of the drug market in terms of sales at final consumption, which to all intents and purposes is the 'street' or 'retail value' (Reuter & Greenfield, 2001, p. 160). While earlier figures provided by analysts like Reuter and Greenfield (2001) are based on landed import price. This is a decent indication of the value of the drug market at the point of trafficking into a country. This may provide a representation of the potential yield for those operating on the production and trafficking end of the spectrum. Developing an estimate of the size and scope of the drug market on an international level is important for a variety of reasons. Different methodologies for gathering data, inconsistencies within data itself, as well as differing priorities for gathering data may all influence the final report.

Overview of the UK Drug Market

In recognition of organised crime conceptualisations and shifts towards market-based organised crime in the criminal underworld, scholarly research would at the turn of the 21st century place increasing emphasis in trying to gauge overall size and structure of Britain's illegal drug market. While the UK government had in the two decades prior frequently published reports on drug harms, studies by May and Hough (2001), Pearson and Hobbs (2001), Pudney et al. (2006) and Casey et al. (2009) would now make concerted effort to establish all-encompassing models indicating how many actors are involved, at which levels and at what financial value and social-economic cost (Reynolds, 2020). Resulting models presented one of two distribution methods, either 'highly structured, pyramidal distribution system' or 'fragmented, non-hierarchical entrepreneurial market with little structure' (May and Hough, 2001, p. 555). Yet, Coomber (2006), among others (See McPhee 2013; McPhee et al., 2019), more recently challenge 'pusher myths' and note in reality most drug transactions occur within social realms between friends, associates and peers, with drugs being sold in open, semi-open or closed markets (Moyle & Coomber, 2015).

While outlining market dynamics, UK scholars have often made efforts to estimate overall drug market value in Britain (Bramley-Harker, 2001; Casey et al., 2009). Levels of difficulty in measurement are considerably reduced when compared to the international context, due to the elimination of issues such as cross-currency analysis, differences in recording practices and differing recording priorities across nations. Still, as with any large-scale data gathering exercise, there remain inconsistencies and discrepancies in the methodology and data, and caution must be applied. As with attempts to establish global drug market worth, UK estimations are also typically dated. The Home Office commissioned work, to be carried out by Pudney et al. (2006), to gather and analyse data over a two-year period Estimations, using supply and demand approaches, were given to be approximately just over £5 billion per annum. As previously stated, the figures stated above, while useful in their representation of the scale of drug use and the amounts generated on a retail level, should be used with caution when valuing the totality of the drug market.

Despite lack of literature pertaining to the areas discussed, there are data available that can provide an insight into the size and scale of the illegal drug market in the United Kingdom. For example, Pudney et al. (2006) estimated the quantity of illegal drugs entering the UK market at that time to be 412 tonnes for cannabis, 20 tonnes for heroin, 18 tonnes for powder cocaine, 16 tonnes for crack and 60 million ecstasy tablets. While these figures represent an estimation based on data gathered 18 years before this writing, overall prevalence of illegal drugs has remained at a similar level in the United Kingdom over this period, and therefore, it is arguable that demand for drugs entering the United Kingdom would also be at a similar level (Black, 2020). In terms of the number of illegal drug seizures conducted, the United Kingdom has the second largest in Europe. First place goes to Spain, which is most likely geographically a main transit point for international drug traffickers (EMCDDA, 2019). The United Kingdom also has one of the largest proportions of cocaine users and high-risk opioid users compared to other EU countries.

The UK illegal drug market is sizeable, in terms of monetary value and scale of retail opportunities. Consequently, the illegal drugs market in the United

Kingdom is extremely competitive and profitable for organised criminal groups (OCGs) trafficking drugs into the country, as well as those at wholesale and retail level distribution (McSweeney et al., 2008). However, since 2018, a number of UK scholars note an 'altered state' in UK supply and demand, whereby technological advances, the use of web orders, saturated drug markets, county lines dealing, emphasis with 'on time' deliveries, among the 'Tinder generation', have seen notable changes in Britain's illegal drug market (Robinson et al., 2019). As suggested by Hales and Hobbs (2010) and Harding (2020), large urban centres like Glasgow, Liverpool and London have become inundated with drug dealers looking to capitalise on the United Kingdom's drug trade. Consequently, markets have become saturated, and this has spilled over into violence in turf and drug wars (Andell and Pitts, 2018; Ruggiero, 2010; Windle and Briggs, 2015).

CHAPTER SUMMARY

This chapter sought to provide the reader with an overview of relevant literature in the area of organised crime and drug markets. While of course both phenomena are vast and to look at all aspects would be beyond the scope of this book alone, efforts have been made to condense and synthesise background material which underpins the rest of the book. As such, the discussion on organised crime itself looked at the terminology and its application given that this has changed significantly over time and has also changed in turn how society comes to consider such phenomena. The literature review then examined drug-related organised crime given the focus of the book, before illumining drug markets more broadly. The next chapter narrows the contextual focus of the study, by considering professional and gang relevant crime in the west of Scotland, and Glasgow more specifically.

3

THE ILLEGAL DRUG TRADE IN WEST SCOTLAND

CHAPTER INTRODUCTION

It is important to emphasise the complex reciprocal relationship between territory and patterns of criminality in Scotland. In their study of the connections between masculinity and environment, Holligan, McLean and Deuchar note the Scottish male identity to be inherently intertwined with the territory in which the male was raised and/or affiliated with (Holligan et al., 2016). This chapter contextualises these connections for readers, highlighting how a multitude of converging variables, not least economy, urban ecology and culture, heavily influenced offending patterns and trends in Scotland.

This chapter opens by justifying the research location of Glasgow as the most appropriate site for exploring changes in Scottish criminal modus operandi towards drug-based organised crime at the professional level. It then briefly overviews the urbanisation of Glasgow, considering the implications of the influx of migrant Irish Catholics into a city/region which had been dominated by Protestantism since the 16th century. Related sectarian tensions, aggravated by a significant economic downturn, led to the manifestation of Glasgow's infamous razor gangs of the 1920/30s. Next, this chapter considers the process of 'social postmodernity' in post-war Glasgow and the rise of territorial 'Young Teams' as razor gang successors. This chapter lastly explores the separation of professional criminals, from gangs per se, reviewing their progression from predatory crimes towards market-based crimes from the 1970s on. This process would set the foundation for the move towards organised criminal groups, concentrated on drug supply, arising with the 1980s heroin boom.

GLASGOW: FORMATION, URBANISATION, INDUSTRIALISATION AND DEINDUSTRIALISATION

Despite changes in Glasgow's post-war housing, industry and administrative boundaries, it retains the status of Scotland's second largest city by area, with the country's largest urban population (and the fourth largest in the United Kingdom overall, behind London, Birmingham and Liverpool – all in England). Glasgow's current population remains relatively stable at just over 60,0000 (Census, 2022). The initial urbanisation of the settlement was driven by 17th century industrialisation. As such, the appeal of work drew large numbers of people from the Scottish Highlands and Ireland. Given that available work was rooted in heavy industry, the city would comprise of a disproportionate number of traditionally working-class populations when compared to Britain's other major cities. Until the 1950s, crime rates and other social ills such as health, substance abuse and prostitution were largely comparable with other leading industrial powerhouses on British shores at the time. Yet the onset of deindustrialisation from the 1970s had a devastating impact. Statistics on crime, health and educational attainment worsened. Glasgow became a significant outlier: a process termed in medical circles as *the Glasgow effect* (Walsh et al., 2010). By the early 2000s, crime rates were three times that of London (in percentage terms). Despite a population less than a 10th that of London, Glasgow had more street gangs than the UK capital (Deuchar, 2013). In 2004, Glasgow had the highest murder rate in Europe, and while murder rates declined since 2015, drug death rates would replace them (Densley et al., 2018). With the exception of a single year, since 2018, Glasgow has consistently had the worse drug harm/death rates of any European city. Indeed, per capita, Glasgow consumes more illegal cocaine than Columbia (BBC, 2019). Yet one should not consider such issues – like violence, murder, gangs and substance misuse – as disparate or disconnected entities. Rather, all are causalities of more deeply embedded components intertwined into Glasgow's very fabric. To fully examine these issues remains outwith the scope of this book alone. But by examining the city's recent history, we can begin to identify and understand some of the key convergent factors which created conditions conducive to drug-based organised crime in Glasgow.

Glasgow was likely founded in the sixth century when Saint Mungo built a church named *Glas Gu* (Lambert, 2023). The then fishing settlement became a small town. Yet, urbanisation of the landscape would halt until Britain's industrial revolution, given that prominent northern European trading routes favoured Scotland's East Coast in the intervening centuries. By the late seventeenth century, Britain industrialised and burgeoning trade routes with North American tobacco colonies resulted in Glasgow's population reaching about 84,000. While writer Daniel Defoe described Glasgow as 'a very fine city' and the centre as 'the... most beautiful... in Britain, London excepted', the reality of housing for the working poor was strikingly different. To relieve overcrowding, new suburbs, like the Gorbals, rapidly developed. Neighbouring towns, like Paisley to Glasgow's south west, also grew significantly at this time due to industrialisation.

By the 19th century, Glasgow had established itself as Second City of the Empire (Gray, 1989). The shipyards were particularly successful. Indeed, the tonnage of ships built in Glasgow rose from 20,000 in 1850 to 5,000,000 in 1900. As Irish migrants and transient Highlanders continued to relocate to Glasgow, the city's population peaked at over one million and just over two million when the wider conurbation was taken into consideration (McLean, 2019a, 2019b, 2019c). The rapid growth of Glasgow outstripped public infrastructure. The disproportionate working-class population lived in densely packed and overcrowded conditions: primarily one and two apartments within four story tenements buildings. Several commissioned reports aimed at addressing poverty found Glasgow's slums to be 'the filthiest' and 'unhealthiest' among British urban settlements (Scott and Hughes, 1980). Cholera outbreaks in 1849 and 1854 killed almost 8,000 people. Infant immortality rates record that half of all children born in the city died before the age of five.

In 1929, Glasgow suffered severe unemployment (Williams, 1994). The Great Depression affected people's lives throughout the 1930s. Shipbuilding was one of the industries hardest hit. While 'the slump' had global effects, in Glasgow, where sectarian division had already been a heated topic, the Irish Catholic immigrants proved easy scapegoats. Significant levels of violence ensued. However, despite the Depression, the city's council (aka Glasgow Corporation) embarked on a large-scale regeneration project. *Slum clearances* saw many communities redeveloped or demolished altogether, while numerous suburbs where built, in an effort to combat poverty and disperse an overcrowded population. The post–World War 2 period saw a revival of industry, and slum clearance projects resumed. However, due to housing demands and financial inflation, projects were amended. Instead of developing 'leafy suburbs', peripheral housing estates begun to resemble dull 'concrete jungles'. Housing tended to comprise of cheaply built three-four story post-war tenements alongside concentrated areas of tower blocks. Alongside the 'Big Four' suburbs – Castlemilk, Drumchapel, Easterhouse and Pollok – a number of 'overspill' towns, like Irvine, East Kilbride and Cumbernauld, were built to rehouse slum populations. Other towns, like Linwood and Johnstone in Renfrewshire, were substantially redeveloped to intake relocated populations.

By 2000, Glasgow had undergone major changes in all areas of life. The slum clearances and overspill policy, alongside boundary reorganisations, saw the population fall to just over half a million (Robertson, 1984). An over-reliance on heavy industry though meant that deindustrialisation impacted significantly upon the population. In one study, Deuchar found it was not uncommon for many households to have suffered second and even third generational unemployment (2009). The economy responded to deindustrialisation with a shift towards the service sector. Scholars of masculinity have identified cultural difficulties in attempts to assimilate once traditionally working-class populations into work perceived as feminine. As previously noted, by the early 2000s, statistics indicated some areas of Glasgow to have rates of violence almost three times that of London. However, since 2015, intense intervention, reinvigorated social and penal strategies, alongside concentrated multi-agency collaborations have all combined to see significant reductions in crime to rates now comparable with other major UK cities.

Paisley, like Glasgow, developed (although originating as a Roman settlement) from an ecclesiastical nucleus, specifically its surviving Cluniac abbey, founded in 1163 (Renfrewshire Council, 2014). By the early 18th century, Paisley had become a manufacturing centre for handloom weaving of linen (MacDonald, 2011, para 9). Its environs also hosted significant shipyards, and from its opening in 1963 to its closure in 1981, its Linwood quarter's manufacturing plant provided cars for a global market, for such brands as Chrysler and Peugeot (The Urban Historian, 2018; Gilmour, 2007). Politically, the town's parliamentary representation is often seen as a 'bellweather' for Scotland and the United Kingdom's shifting electoral allegiances. In his guise as a novelist, Victorian Conservative prime minister Benjamin Disraeli famously wrote 'keep your eye on Paisley', and the United Kingdom's last Liberal premier, Herbert Henry Asquith, was the town's MP from 1920 to 1924 (MacDonald, 2011, *passim*). The United Kingdom's shortest serving (Conservative) prime minister, Liz Truss, made much of her early childhood (1979–1985, aged approximately four to 10 before moving to Roundhay, Leeds) in the town, while her parents taught at what is now the University of the West of Scotland's Paisley Campus (Paterson, 2022). As is seen below, Paisley's struggles with deindustrialisation left it especially prone to drug-related organised crime. This association with organised crime and poverty is even juxtaposed by the current Renfrewshire Council as a key premise of its urban regeneration strategy and related funding appeals, as Conor Wilson (2024) has shown.

Deindustrialisation in Scotland has been helpfully characterised by Phillips, Wright and Tomlinson (2019) as 'a process not an event'. It was managed relatively sensitively (i.e. with restructuring, closures and redeployment negotiated with workers' trades union and political representatives) by successive Labour and Conservative UK governments in the 1960s and 1970s and 'recklessly' (laissez-faire) by the 1980s Conservative Thatcher governments (Gibbs, 2018). Between 1962 and 1988, industrial employment (i.e. males and females in occupations including manufacturing, coal mining and construction) fell markedly from 46.7% to 28%. The decline between 1962 and 1978 had been gradual (46.7% to 38%), whereas that between 1978 and 1988 – broadly mirroring the three terms of Margaret Thatcher's (1979–1990) premiership – had been precipitous (38% to 28%) (Phillips et al., 2019, pp. 151–2). Gibbs (2021) and Clark (2021, 2023) have written extensively about the complex impacts of deindustrialisation on individual and community identities. This includes a joint article on these themes (2020).

Parallel to the socio-economic dislocation wrought by deindustrialisation in the 1980s and 1990s, Scottish local government was in the 1970s and then again in the 1990s radically reorganised in ways which made the new local authority structures democratically, and often physically, remote from the communities they administered (Pugh, 2014, 2016). Running parallel to these changes was a process of 'hollowing out' of the local state's responsibilities in favour of private enterprise and voluntarism (Rhodes, 1994). Pugh (2014, 2016) and Pugh with Connolly (2016) have explored this process and its ramifications in the Scottish context, and the current book elaborates it with specific and significant reference to criminogenesis. The most recent manifestations of hollowing out in the Scottish context centre on contracting out of local non-statutory services, like culture and leisure, to 'arms-length' bodies outwith local government's direct control, alongside the Community Empowerment Act (2015), which *inter alia* enables community bodies to take over and operate council facilities in their own interest. Pugh and Connolly (2014) have questioned the extent to which this is genuine empowerment so much as responsibilisation of vulnerable communities for their own predicaments, but were not cognisant of the potential for the legislation to be abused by organised crime groups. Somewhat ironically in this context, they wrote that the legislation could be hijacked by 'more established interest groups', albeit they did not have organised crime groups specifically in mind. This more sinister potential is clearly implied in the episodes this book relates below, of council resources being quite literally handed over to organised crime groups in Paisley and north Glasgow. As is seen as a recurring theme below, the dislocations caused by deindustrialisation and local democratic disengagement proved fertile soil for drug-related organised crime more broadly.

CITY OF GANGS

Understanding how Glasgow was created is particularly important for ultimately understanding how crime came to express itself first within the city, then across the region and eventually throughout Scotland. As noted, Glasgow's industrial urbanisation coincided with the relocation of large numbers of indigenous Protestant Highlanders and migrant Catholics from Ireland. The 1841 census identified Scotland's Irish-born population at 126,321, yet a decade later, this rose 90% to 207,367, from a total population of 2,888,742. Yet, the population was far from being equally dispersed. Scotland's industrial west coast would have the largest concentration, with almost 30% of all Irish migrants settling in Glasgow. During 1848, it was estimated that between January and April alone, 42,860 Irish people would settle in the city (Handley, 2001). The influx had a profound effect on the city's social life. Catholic Irish populations tended to settle in homogeneous communities: often running adjacent to those communities of the indigenous Protestant Scottish population (Davies, 2013). Close proximity, increased competition in the labour market, impoverishment and conflicting religious ideology, all contributed to sectarian tension (Handley, 1950, p. 100). Furthermore, protestant churches actively encouraged anti-Catholic feelings: helping to institutionalise sectarianism. Sectarian hatred would also be expressed through sports: most notably in the creation of the Protestant Rangers Football Club and the Catholic Celtic Football Club. Even as late as 1923, the Church of Scotland published the pamphlet *The Menace of the Irish Race to our Scottish Nationality* (Handley, 2001). Tensions would ultimately turn violent, particularly in the wake of the 1929 Great Depression.

Many of the skilled indigenous protestant work force blamed the Catholic Irish for economic recession, by providing a cheap alternative source of unskilled labour. From this resentment, Glasgow's infamous razor gangs were born. Davies' book *City of Gangs* (2013) reviews, in considerable detail, the manifestation of razor gangs and explores how knife crime became entrenched into the fabric of social life at the time. Davies argues while street gangs, such as the Penny Mobs, had existed as far back as the mid-19th century, razor gangs were markedly different. While Penny Mobs comprised youths engaged in theft, essentially to feed themselves. Razor gangs on the other hand tended to span the age range and were products of social unrest: serving recreational, political and financial needs. Davies presents a case study of two of the most infamous razor gangs at the time: the Protestant based Bridgeton Derry Boys and the Roman Catholic based Norman Conks. Close geographical proximity, in the city's East End, ensured clashes were regular. The Bridgeton Derry Boys' charismatic leader Billy Fullerton was a staunch protestant and demanded his gang adopt militaristic style behaviour. This included dedicated fighting units, marching bands, holding regular parades, paying fees and adopting a strict dress code. The gang were held in esteem in the local community and, as such, attracted many youths. The gang therefore created a junior section, the Derry Boys. This ingrained gang doctrine and sectarian hatred in future generations. The Conks, and others, would respond in kind. Tracing the historical development of contemporary Young Teams in Glasgow, McLean notes these junior outfits laid the blueprint for the subsequent territorial street gangs of the post-war period (McLean, 2019a, 2019b, 2019c). This process had two stages.

McLean (2019a, 2019b, 2019c) suggested territoriality among Young Teams could neither be traced solely to feudal clan mentality nor imperial military regiment competitiveness. Rather, McLean suggests hyper-territorial behaviour as the product of razor gangs using territoriality as a mechanism to identify religious and ethnic differences. Given Catholics tended to be of Irish decent and Protestants of Scottish descent, each group residing within particular neighbourhood boundaries, location signified ethno-religious identity. Gangs could be assured random attacks within certain communities would likely be perpetrated upon those of particular religious and/or ethnic affiliation. Indeed, Glasgow gang names tended to, and still do, have religious or sectarian prefix or suffix, such as Derry, Shamrock, Bhoys and similar followed by the relevant housing estate name.[1] One example is Bridgeton (estate) Derry (religious). Religious affiliations and entrenched territoriality remained key features of post-war street gangs.

The second stage of the process of gangs' historical development was that knife crime became entrenched into fighting culture in Glasgow, the razor gangs' legacy. Davies points to American gangsterism, as projected on the then increasingly popular pastime of visiting the cinema, as having a profound effect in the city (1998, 2013). At the time, particular emphasis was placed on recognising such practice as being a 'shameful', even (with clear racist overtones) 'negro', activity. Yet, using knives when fighting nonetheless gained prominence among Glasgow's emerging razor gangs. Davies suggests this may be due to the level of sectarian hatred and also because slashing a victim's face acted as a stark warning to others not to challenge the gangs.

As well as the case study of the Derry and Conks, Davies published several earlier articles on the Beehive Boys, from Glasgow's Gorbals district. Unlike the gangs of the East End, the Beehive Boys took their name from a pub on a

---

1 The prefix Derry Boys is adopted from the Apprentice Boys of Derry who are a Protestant fraternal society founded in 1814 in the city of Derry, Northern Ireland.

street corner: arguably due to having a more ethnic and religiously diverse population, comprising of Catholics, protestants and Jews from Ireland, Scotland and Italy. This makes the gang somewhat unique, yet the Beehive Boys still nonetheless affiliated with more religiously entrenched razor gangs. Davies notes while gang fights were frequent, and often public spectacles, at times comprising of several hundred individuals, razor gangs tended to also have a small close-knit group of core offenders at the centre, whom other outer members would associate with. Former Gangland enforcer, turned author, Jimmy Boyle (1977) notes for most razor gang, association was dependent upon circumstances as members tended to drift in and out of affiliation, with a consistent core membership (Matza, 1964).

The core body was permanent, as 1930s gang fighting police chief Sir Percy Sillitoe (1888–1962) noted in his memoirs (1956). The core body comprised persistent offenders (Farrington et al., 2006): characterised as intrinsically criminal. While the core body would engage in territorial violence, they would also engage in frequent criminal activity centred on acquiring monetary value. This would include using the wider gang as a means for racketeering, providing muscle for hire, taxing other local criminals and predatory-based crimes such as jewellery heists, armed robbery and safe cracking. Examining the case of the Beehive Boys, Davies attributes such behaviour to the fact that core members tended to be older and likewise, during the economic depression, used the gang as a means for sustaining income to support dependants. In the preceding decades following the World War 2, the razor gangs would diminish. While Sillitoe's aggressive and heavy-handed police tactics are often credited in official circles with much of the demise of the razor gangs, it is unlikely to have been a sole or even main deciding factor. Explanations that are more plausible are given by Davies, who points to the start of Britain's war with Germany in 1939, as well as wide-scale social reforms, slum clearances and post-war economic revival thereafter. Yet following the end of the war in 1945, the post-war reconstruction of Glasgow saw inner-city gang culture extrapolated further afield via the city's overspill policy and the widening of cultural pastimes and technological advances, as noted in Johanne Miller's PhD thesis *In Every Scheme there is a Team* (2015). While the pre-war era belonged to the razor gangs, the post-war era would see a split between what was once the core membership of razor gangs and junior outfits, into professional criminals and Young Teams. McLean (2019a, 2019b, 2019c) argues that while razor gangs were a product of industrialisation, inner-city urbanisation and economic recession, the post-war professional criminal groups and territorial youth gangs were a product of deindustrialisation, suburban living in poorly planned resettlement programmes, and the shift from masculine based work to perceived feminine types of employment.

SEPARATING MEN FROM BOYS

The year 1945 brought many changes to Britain. Social, economic, political and cultural changes would equally span both the upper and underworld. After the war, Britain entered into a period of rebuilding and social engineering. Universal healthcare was established, the superstructure of the contemporary welfare state had been implemented and heavy industry, once again, proved the backbone of British economy (McIvor & Johnston, 2004). The slum clearances, along with the completion of massive peripheral estates, resulted in the relocation of much of the population (McLean, 2019a, 2019b, 2019c). On the one hand, this period of urban reconstruction helped, along with fighting oversees common enemies, break down entrenched sectarian barriers – at least to some degree in that communities became mixed – but on the other hand, such rapid change created a whole new set of problems. Moulded in the image of self-functioning towns, these new estates were characterised by: poorly built post-war tenement housing or tower blocks, few amenities or recreational facilities, lacking local employment opportunities and inadequate transport to established areas of inner-city work. The populations of these estates had already been typically poor but were now marginalised, isolated and largely forgotten. Deindustrialisation of the city's heavy industry in coming years would only serve to accelerate such processes. Indeed, the shift towards a service sector thereafter provoked a masculinity crisis among young men. No longer able to express masculinity through employment, young men did so on the streets: typically manifested via gang violence (Rafanell et al., 2017).

It had been hoped Glasgow's new estates would rid the city of the crime and other social ills that had longed plagued inner-city slums. Reviewing media construction of gang narratives, historical gang expert Angela Bartie (2010) notes large estates with clear boundary lines allowed board youths in isolated housing estates to engage in territorial battles with youth living in nearby neighbouring estates. Linguistic and printed narratives among media, local authorities, law enforcement and the political establishment though gradually leant itself towards moral panics over the re-emergence of gang culture from 1965 to 1970. Yet, gang narratives, this time, would be applied solely to youth groups engaged in recreational violence over territory. McLean (2019a,

2019b, 2019c) notes the extrapolation of earlier inner-city knife culture, from the bygone era of razor gangs, to raise its ugly face again and lend new menace to Young Team inter-scheme battles. McLean argues intergenerational narratives of lived, and shared, history by former razor gang members, now parents and grandparents, would tell stories of their past glories to younger generations. The older generation would act as role models for the younger generations, whom lacking the organisational skillset needed to create militaristic or profit-seeking criminal enterprises, instead adopted, and replicated, those easily assimilated practice and features from their predecessors. This included knife carrying, defending territoriality, and adopting gang signs, linguistics, and symbols. Consequently, such behaviour coincided with the new application of gang terminology, in the Glasgow, and later Scottish context, through gang talkers in media outlets, political circles and public debates, to those young territorial street gangs (Hallsworth & Young, 2008).

As media and police evermore used gang terminology to describe Young Teams, such terminology no longer fitted with groups of persistent adult offenders, which would have once been core members of razor gangs. Those in positions of authority needed a new way to distinguish gangs of youths from now distinct entities of adult criminals. With the exception of a few criminal groups, such as the XYY gang (see Jeffrey, 2011) - a term given by police and media to indicate their lack of knowledge on assailant identity - most adult criminal groups, tended to be family-based, and thus became known by the surname of the eldest member, leader, or most prominent public figure. Notable examples in Britain include the Krays, the Richardsons and in Glasgow the Thompson crime family, located in the city's East End, headed by Arthur Thompson senior (McKay, 2006b). For these professionals, the new post-war landscape would become their domain. The recently constructed periphery housing estates were truly massive in size and in addition housed anywhere between 30,000 to 50,000 people (Damer, 2018). Most were completed by the early 1960s. Yet, typically, only a dozen or so police officers would be charged with policing the estate at any given time (Rannoc, 2019). Logistics would prove difficult. Criminals, like the XYY gang, would be tipped off by insiders on business payrolls, as to when and where wages would be sent. Isolated post offices on these estates proved easy targets for criminal groups to conduct armed robbery (Jeffery, 2011).

While predatory crimes had long existed, by the 1970s, criminals on these estates made headway into market-based crimes. Advances in technology, communication and a more professionalised system of police and security made robbery all the more difficult. The invention and greater use of silent alarms, the two-way fitted radio, home telephones, mobilised police units, armed response units and the digitalisation of currency necessitated this shift. For the underworld, globalisation and international supply chains meant market-based crimes had greater potential for success, sustainability and carried less risk (Von Lampe, 2016). Criminal organisations like the Russian mafia, the Cosa Nostra and the Aryan Brotherhood tend to opportunistically fill voids left behind by inadequately regulated legitimate society. As with Levi (2016), who identified the illegal supply of western white and electronic goods into the former Soviet Union, by Russian Mafioso, in Glasgow, the creation of large periphery estates lacking the essential amenities enabled criminal opportunity. From the late 1960s until the late 1980s, the newly developed urban ecological landscape created by Glasgow council, along with the creation and growth of poorly regulated markets in couriering, private security, to name a few, produced ideal conditions for professional criminals to flourish. Although somewhat shrined in secrecy, given illegality, a handful of investigative journalists, autobiographical accounts and insider accounts recall efforts by professional criminals to enter unregulated markets in the taxi service, private security firms, and ice-cream distribution, in Glasgow.

Transport in, around, and out of these estates was essential, and as such, the taxi industry grew exponentially during the late 1960s and more so the 1970s. The widespread use of landline telephones allowed direct communication to taxi offices, thus aiding the development of taxi firms. Glasgow had traditionally used London-style black cabs as its official taxi fleet. Taxicabs were maintained to a high standard. Likewise, drivers were required to be vetted before being allowed to operate. Yet as demand outstripped supply, pirate taxi firms began to emerge during the 1970s. Pirate cabs tended to lack necessary paperwork, operate poorly maintained vehicles, avoid proper council and police checks and have no insurance. While, the market remained unregulated for well over a decade, it would be 1982, before policy changes adequately begun to address the situation. Such change was largely the result of pirate firms' encroachment evermore within the city centre itself: consequently, reducing custom for official black cabs. The Civic Government (Scotland) Act 1982 thus sought to legitimise pirate cabs, as prior efforts to halt the trade had failed miserably. The introduction of the law meant Scotland now had another tier in public transport, called Private Hire. New laws meant private hires now had to be vetted by local councils, with driver's receiving a licence, corresponding number and fitted plates.

However, while much improved, even after 1982, the taxi service still remained unregulated. The handling of hard currency meant criminals were able to still manipulate the system, as well as exploiting new opportunities. Tam 'The Licensee' McGraw had been a notable professional criminal, working alongside infamous figures such as T. C. Campbell and Billy, carrying out predatory crimes like theft, burglary and armed robbery on factories, jewellery shops and post offices (McKay, 2010). Yet, increasing difficulties and risk around predatory crimes, alongside the new opportunities presented in market-based crime, saw McGrew move towards private taxi hire. Using reputation and criminal networks, McGrew would use muscle – McPhee, Tamby and Campbell – to intimidate other private hire firms, in an effort to either cease operating on certain estates or be brought under his ownership. Although lacking physical stature, McGraw was intelligent, anti-surveillance aware and self-educated in business and law. Placing all ownership of business under his wife's name, McGrew knew, under Scottish Law, a wife could not be forced to testify against her husband. Such shrewd moves kept him ahead of competitors. Others, like Steven Malcolm, now one of Scotland wealthiest businessmen, built his fortune from owning private taxi hire companies. Like McGraw, Malcolm used underworld contacts in Paisley to intimidate and vandalise the property of others both in legal and illegal taxi firms. Such tactics saw criminals like Malcolm and McGraw gain notable monopolisation of first illegal then legal taxi firm businesses (Findlay, 2018).

Following the explosion of the drug trade in the late 1980s, the private hire firms would be used to hide, and launder, drug money. Indeed, several early notable traffickers exploited private hire services to directly transport drugs, and dealers alike, to make drop offs and collections across Scotland and England. Drivers would be paid a daily rate and would thus be associates of professional criminals. Others, such as Stuart Boyd, likewise used taxi services to their benefit. Any illegal goods identified by police could be attributed to the driver, the passenger(s) or previous passengers who may have forgotten or had to ditch commodities for whatever given or preconceived reason. Taxi drivers could likewise account for large figures of hard currency (McLean, 2024).

While the creation of periphery housing estates without amenities created opportunities for criminals to enter the taxi service, other opportunities in similar unregulated industries begun to emerge. In Glasgow, none is perhaps more infamous than that of ice-cream vans. Much of the ice-cream wars is shrouded in mystery with a number of stabbing and murders – none more notable than that of six Doyle family members by way of arson attack on the Cranhill estate in 1984 – remaining outstanding (McLean, 2018). Yet Teddy Rannoc (2019) – a former van driver turned author – identifies the process through which McGraw would muscle in on the van trade. In the early 1980s, the Marchetti Brothers owned much of the legitimate ice-cream vans on the streets of Glasgow. However, given that the market was largely unregulated and the periphery housing estates were vast spaces with few shops and with fewer police to cover the area, the van trade was ideal for criminals to muscle in on. McGraw would set up the initial fees for loose associates to rent purchased ice-cream vans which he would then allocate an area to operate within. The drivers would remain the legitimate face of the operation in order to avoid licences being revoked. McGraw and associates would then systematically target van drivers and smash up other local vans operated in the area. Yet division among McGraw and those in the close-knit circle of associates resulted in the landscape being divvied up. Rannoc claims the link between ice-cream vans and drug distribution to be an image projected by media who understood little about the feud. It is possible with time, vans were used to launder and hide drug money, but given the steps that McGraw and others took to keep their own vans clean on the surface, it is unlikely drugs were sold directly from vans given police could impound vehicles with little notice and did so regularly. Several commentaries, including officers of the then 'Flying Squad', Scotland's police unit dedicated to addressing serious crimes in the county, in the two part BBC documentary covering the ice-cream wars, likewise support claims that no drugs were ever sold or suspected of being sold from the vans.

Another notable area of industry in which criminals begun to muscle in on from the 1980s onwards was private security. A number of professional criminals would use their prior reputations as local hard-men or as armed robbers, with access to firearms and a reputation for violence, to enter the security trade. The market was, like the taxi businesses and ice-cream trade, undergoing considerable growth in the new world of modernity and free market policies, in Glasgow's evolving landscape. Private security was largely unregulated, and with the number of housing estates undergoing development via urban regeneration, security firms were required to guard access to work premises, and to the equipment and materials which had to be left on construction sites overnight. Again, professional criminals would gradually use their reputation to enter this marketplace. Given that construction sites were often large and poorly guarded meant that criminals could pay associates to vandalise such premises, causing considerable damage to both the value and reputation of well-established security forms. As a result, matters would often be settled outside of the legitimate sphere with criminals, such as Paul Ferris, John Healy and Stuart Boyd, all using their reputations as gangland enforcers to enter the scene.

A number of police probes and proposal would indicate that the matter was largely due to cash-in-hand transactions and poorly defined regulations, coupled with the ability to exploit loopholes in growing market based industries, as being the main cause for criminal entry into such areas of work.

Since these areas of the economy have been increasingly regulated, others have opened up in the modern society, including nail bars, tanning salons and other areas of the beauty industry. However, perhaps most notable in the Glasgow scene with the rise of the professional criminal was that of Arthur Thompson Senior. Having made a considerable reputation as a safe cracker and armed robber, Thompson would use knowledge gained from underworld connections and time spent in prison, to reassess criminal enterprise. Making a move towards racketeering, extortion and entry into a number of areas of emerging markets such as taxis and security, Thompson recognised the lure of the growing drug market. A pioneer in this area, Thompson would use connections to a number of underworld contacts to secure supply lines and provide local customers. Yet, Thompson became embroiled in a gangland feud with former enforcer Paul Ferris after the murder of his son Arthur 'Fatboy' Thompson Jnr. Like Thompson, numerous autobiographical accounts from those such as Stephen French (Johnson, 2007) or Bernard O'Mahoney (2003) note that professional criminals tended to capture the imagination and dominate the criminal landscape through robbery and heists. Yet, globalisation coupled with increased technology, surveillance and policing methods meant that the risk-reward ratio provided by predatory crime was simply not worth it. Market-based opportunities instead would provide lucrative areas to move into in the new period of modernity. Using reputation, access to violence and firearms and criminal networks, predatory criminals could move into such markets or provide muscle for those who did so.

CHAPTER SUMMARY

This chapter contextualised Glasgow's criminal evolution prior to the 1980s heroin boom. The discussion was twofold, showing that urban and economic changes shape the social and cultural environment in both legitimate society and the criminal underworld. By outlining the urbanisation, industrialisation and deindustrialisation of the landscape and discussing how global processes affect the local environment in post-war society, a process often term the 'glocal' (Mares, 1999, p. 139) indicates how particular types of criminality emerged. The change in post-war gang narratives, once seen as a single entity comprising youths, recreational participants in violence and professional criminals alike, became two distinct and separate entities. Gang terminology was confined to youths, while adults were labelled professionals in the eyes of law enforcement and the political establishment. Professionals were referred to with the collective prefix of the surname of the most prominent figure, followed by a descriptive group suffix, i.e. 'team' 'crew' 'boys', etc. in media and public circles.

This chapter then discussed how changes apropos globalisation and internationalisation of trade, alongside increased technology in surveillance and policing, resulted in a reduction of opportunities to engage in predatory crime, incentivising market-based crime. Criminals began opportunistically entering unregulated and poorly constructed legal markets during the 1970s and 1980s. This process fits with wider discussions of international criminal outfits. Yet, as is seen in the coming chapters, following the second wave of heroin in the late 1980s, professional criminals in Scotland concentrated on drug markets and would later be coined organised crime groups in fitting with Americanised international doctrine. Wider literature on organised crime in Britain, including discussions of the Brinks-Mat robbery, whereby the theft of gold was used to help facilitate sustained criminal operations in drug markets, indicate a notable change in organised criminal behaviour from the late 1980s to the early 1990s.

4

GANG REORGANISATION AROUND DRUG NETWORKS, 1980–1994

CHAPTER INTRODUCTION

Having introduced the background of the study, overviewed the academic literature and outlined Glasgow's criminal development, this book now examines how traffickers in Scotland affected subsequent gang reorganisation. While traffickers had been importing various types of drugs and other illicit goods into the country long before the 1980s, to varying degrees, an emergent trafficker class would come to the fore around this period. They supplied drugs, in vast bulk, into an expanding and evermore demanding marketplace; this trade's value was estimated as several million pounds. This provided a significant incentive for criminals to get involved. It led professional gangs of criminals to change their operations reorganising specifically around drug supply, heroin in particular. This drug had the most significant impact on the country's criminal scene. This chapter opens by examining a few key actors and how they became involved in drug supply, analysing how growing drug markets, demand and supply would impact upon gang reorganisation and subsequent drug wars.

MR P AND FORGING SUPPLYING ROUTES INTO PAISLEY

Counterintuitively, despite Glasgow's long and synonymous history with gangs, our story of early drug trafficking does not begin inside its city boundaries, but rather in its by then neighbouring (south-west) town of Paisley. It was Paisley where Scottish criminals begin to depart from their predecessors' patterns as professional opportunistic outfits centred on predatory crimes like armed robbery, theft and bank heists, instead reorganising themselves around the booming illicit drugs trade. In the process they became highly organised criminal groups specialising in narcotics. This story cannot be told without discussing the man who would later be coined 'last man standing' following a decade long gangland war in Paisley, which left at least 14 people dead and many more wounded (Findlay, 2012a).

Despite being long involved in criminality, K's first adult criminal conviction was in 1985, when he was aged 29 years.[1] Then, he received a seven-year prison sentence for the supply of cannabis resin. Upon his early release, K resumed his position in the criminal underworld. As a result, he would later be convicted for drug trafficking, cannabis and amphetamines, on 27 September 1993 (The Herald, 1993b). He was handed a three-year sentence. A further charge on firearms would see K convicted again in 2004. This life of crime was very different from his early aspirations to become a professional sporting personality. Once a promising young footballer, having had a relatively successful stint as a prolific centre forward at Airdrie United Football Club, in little over a decade, K would gain the unofficial title 'Mr P', an abbreviation of Mr Paisley, in acknowledgement of his rule over the town's criminal underworld (Alexander, 2017). Raised in Ferguslie Park, the deprived post-war housing scheme, K first drew on the same young men of his generation, with whom he would later become embroiled in bitter rivalry with in the drugs trade, to help him carve out a fearsome reputation as a local 'hard man' and renowned fighter.

By 1970, the sectarian razor gangs were long gone, yet, as is seen, their legacy created a blueprint for an even more formidable challenge for Scottish law enforcement. The razors' junior fighting outfits, which once provided the young men of the city a quasi-militaristic outlet to demonstrate their fighting prowess and masculinity, had been replaced with more volatile, knife wielding, youth groups, or 'Young Teams', engaged in hyper-masculine recreational gang violence. Young teams had no purpose beyond inflicting damage, causing trouble and fighting for fighting's sake. Defined by engrained cultural territorialism, Young Teams, with an identifying suffix of their eponymous housing estates, saw large groups of boys, some as young as 12 years of age armed with weapons and bladed instruments, to battle weekly on the streets (McLean, 2019a, 2019b, 2019c). Many a young man, adolescent, boy or even

---

1 The information on K provided throughout this chapter is primarily gathered from media sources and information given by interviewees without any one single source. The authors have refrained from providing specific quotations from interviewees in order to protect their identities.

child died as a result. At 13 years of age, K excelled in the fighting, and revelled in the status and – often academically overlooked – social aspect of brotherhood that it brought among peers (Deuchar, 2009).

His time as a gang member of the Feegie Young Team, or Feegie Pandas, saw him acquire a formidable reputation that would later be utilised forging a drugs empire in the criminal underworld. Although raised in a good home, with loving parents and a younger sibling, the gang fighting resulted in K being removed from the family home and placed in Scotland's Borstal system, where, like in adult prisons, criminogenic skills were more often honed than kerbed. In reality, for all their fearsome reputation as being a place of future hard men, these institutions were places of punitive authoritarianism, harm and abuse. Many a report in later years illumined the extent and magnitude, of widespread institutionalised harm.[2] A system that was intended to nurture young men back towards social integration only served to catapult them further away. Many a young boy who entered the system would return to the streets a hardened criminal; often with significant post-traumatic stress. The system also had unintended consequences of providing its residents with a web of delinquent/criminal contacts. This resource was one which K fully exploited in his mid-to-late adolescent years.

Upon his release from Borstal, K acquired a social house from the local council at 16 years of age, in 1972. His house was situated on St James Street, somewhat ironically directly opposite the town's sheriff court, a place K and his associates would come frequent. K had been offered other properties around the town, including one in his scheme of origin, Ferguslie Park, but had purposefully sought the location in St James Street, given its proximity to the town centre. K had dual intentions for the house. It would prove a hub not only for socialising and nightlife, as night club revellers made their way to and from the town centre's bustling night-time economy, but also for furthering his ambition to create a criminal enterprise. It further served as a safe house, used by K's criminogenic peers, as they exploited the opportunities the town centre provided for theft and robbery. The house proved the perfect hideout, situated close by, for those who had stolen goods and sought to disappear, and lay low, following a criminal act, until the heat was off. K would not only provide temporary refuge to these 'players' but would use his contacts through the Young Team and Borstal system, to move on recently stolen goods, for a fee or favour of course. It was during this time K acquired a reputation as a good intermediary for obtaining and moving stolen goods. Interviewee Shirley states:

---

2 For example, those reports produced by The Historical Institutional Abuse enquiry.

> [K]'s house was close to the town. My older brother would often thieve from the shops and go to [K]'s to hide it. I think K sold it on to other people for him. He was a go to type of guy if you wanted something.

Influenced by the wave of new charismatic and even rebellious genres of art and music, the subcultural movement of 1960s also resulted in the popularity of cannabis use, particularly among British youths (Parker, 2000). By the late 1970s, cannabis use was embedded in certain social circles in the United Kingdom. Again, K would use his house to good effect. Initially, by way of socialising, K would host after parties at his home after nights out on the town. Alcohol and cannabis were regularly consumed. K himself begun to buy cannabis to consume and give to those attending the house parties. Noticing the growing popularity of the drug, he would quickly move from operating as a social supplier to a retail level dealer, and then as a wholesaler. Again, K's contacts in the criminal underworld were leveraged. Unlike many low-level suppliers, K was able to buy in bulk and thus increase profits while cutting out the middleman (McPhee, 2013). As such, K was able to secure a steady flow of drugs, with increasing sums of money going in the opposite direction.

During his early experiences of 'moving on' stolen goods, K learnt that it was better to shift such commodities on to buyers and intermediaries outside the county, and if possible the country all together. In addition to reducing the risk of being caught by law enforcement, moving stolen goods further afield to be redistributed also meant there was a reduced chance that would-be buyers would recognise their own stolen goods now being sold on, or for other local criminals trying to muscle in on the trade. K exploited extended kinship networks in criminal families in London both to sell goods and to purchase drugs. Giving K an advantageous position over others trying to operate in the growing trade, was the fact that a close relative, had in the late 1970s, moved to the Netherlands. Having lived briefly with K, while on the run from the law, his relative formed a close bond with him. Sheltering his relative, he was able to establish trust; something which mafia expert Jack Katz highlights, in his (1988) book *Seductions of Crime*, as a much-needed resource for any would-be criminal to operate at the higher echelons of the underworld. Once in the Netherlands, his relative exploited *laissez-faire* drug laws in the country's largest city, Amsterdam, to access large quantities of cannabis to ship to the United Kingdom, into London, before transporting it onwards to Scotland. Historian Stephen Snelders (2021) points out that Netherlands' intact postcolonial infrastructure created the perfect transport hub for the movement of goods from central Europe into Western Europe and Britain; something K knew all too well.

Initially, K would regularly collect shipments himself; more for the thrill, than to boost profit. In his later years, K would use his personal courier system to do so to avoid detection and reduce risk, as evidenced in the conviction of Edward King, in 1993 (Herald, 1993a). The Herald, 8th December 1993, reports that King was arrested transporting 125 kg of cannabis resin from London to Paisley, after being clocked travelling at speeds of up to 110 mph in his hire car along the M74 on 8 December 1992. Although King confessed to being a courier, the buyer, suspected as K, was never identified. K peddled explicitly in cannabis resin at this point, something his criminal appeals application, 1984, would evidence when charged with distributing across the Renfrewshire district (Scottish Courts & Tribunals, 1986).

By the mid-1980s Scotland still had few high-end wholesalers and even less large-scale drug importers. It was unsurprising, then, that Police in the close-knit town of Paisley, with a population then of approximately 90,000, were able to quickly identify K as the among its few high-end drug traffickers. A police surveillance operation was set up to uncover the extent of his network. Again, K's petition to the court of appeals, albeit under the alternative spelling of his second name, McIntosh, it is evident he had built a considerable network of cannabis supply. Operating out of the popular 'Abercorn Bar', K would move cannabis on to would-be buyers at both wholesale and retail level transactions. The document shows:

> *The accused were concerned in the supply of controlled drugs namely cannabis resin and amphetamine, both class B drugs, in contravention of sec. 4 (1) of the said Act. The allegation was that this had occurred between 24th August 1983 and 3rd May 1985 at the following places, namely Glasgow Airport, Paisley; 48 Penilee Road, Paisley; the Abercorn Bar, Gauze Street, Paisley; 12 Almond Crescent, Paisley; H.M. Prison, Lowmoss, Bishopbriggs; H.M. Prison, Dungavel, Strathaven; 11 Clarence Street, Paisley; 13 Clarence Street, Paisley; 47 Glencairn Drive, Glasgow; and elsewhere in Paisley and Glasgow. Scottish Courts and Tribunals (1986)*

K's appeal would subsequently be partially accepted that he was received lesser convictions in exchange for a guilty plea. He was nonetheless sentenced to seven years imprisonment. During his time incarcerated in Barlinnie Prison, Glasgow, K would form a strong alliance with another key actor in the drugs trade. Arthur 'Arty' Thompson Junior, son of Arthur 'godfather' Thompson

Senior, head of the Thompson crime family, who had extensive criminal networks across Glasgow and the West (McKay, 2007). K formed a good friendship with Arthur Jnr, as recalled by reformed gangland enforcer; turned author and TV personality, Paul Ferris. While dismissive of the duo as a formidable force, Ferris nonetheless notes the close extent of this friendship bond between either party in his memoirs, *The Ferris Conspiracy*, (Ferris & McKay, 2001). He recalled K and Arty drawing upon Quentin Tarantino's Hollywood film *Reservoir Dogs'* humourous dialect, when interacting with one another over a series of telephone calls (Ferris & McKay, 2001). In an exclusive interview with investigative journalist Ron Moore, as part of the *News of the World's, Crime Scene* series, in 2011, K revealed the pair didn't do 'business' with one another, but did have 'some adventures'. This statement's ambiguity was intended. In a series of letter exchanges, between 2020 and 2022, with a Barlinnie inmate, and K's right-hand man, by the name of Derek Steven Brockwell (dubbed 'Britain's most dangerous criminal' having stabbed several prison officers following a jailbreak), K states he and Arthur Jnr did indeed operate regular business exchanges with one another (BBC, 2018a). While discussing the 'bad blood' between K, Brockwell and Thompson on one side and Ferris and co. on the other, K writes 'Young Arty (Thompson Jnr) was always easy to work with'. The role of K and Arthur Jnr in forging drug supply routes into Paisley cannot be overstated. These supply routes, and ensuing criminal networks, contributed significantly to criminal groups in Paisley, and later Glasgow and the West, reorganising to specialise in the drugs trade.

Given proximity, and intergenerational kinship extending across the town and city, Paisley and Glasgow have since industrialisation been intertwined, in the legal and illegal spheres. As his ventures in the illicit drugs trade increased, K continually reorganised those relevant networks used for moving stolen goods towards trafficking cannabis, and later amphetamines. While not directly involved in supplying opioids, these same routes forged by K would, nonetheless, be exploited by other connected underworld associates, to move heroin. Having allied himself with Glasgow's most powerful crime family, via Arthur Jnr, K proved pivotal in creating future drug supply links between Glasgow and Paisley. Another important factor in this process was not only K's criminal networking, but also his ability to act as an intermediary in settling disputes between powerful underworld figures. Criminologist Peter Reuter points to the mafia's ability to connect potential businesses partners in the legal and illegal realm as the feature of central importance in enabling success. Historian John Dickie develops this theme, pointing to the ability of *Mafiosi* to carry 'violence capital' (i.e. viewing criminal violence as a form of social action) as equally important (2007, 2012). K demonstrates both traits in creating and forging business links, as well as using reputation, and contacts, to express subtle volatile undertones. Indeed written correspondence, dated 15 February 2021, between K and Brockwell, point to this position of prestige. In the letter, Brockwell recalls the event for a third party, stating of K:

> *He is man of great standing in Paisley.... K dominated the Paisley scene for many years because [of] his reputation for getting things done, and seeing off rivals.*

Proceeding, Brockwell recalls K's ability to facilitate meetings between highly volatile figures, in this case between Brockwell and Ferris[3]:

> *[K] had a phone call from an underworld figure called The Ferrit[4] wanting to know if he knew a big lump of a guy who went by the name Brocky. [K] knew the Ferrit from a previous prison sentence in the 80s' and summarised there was something aloof [afoot]... [Ferrit] asked for a meet?... [K] arranged for a sit down... [The meeting itself] was getting heated, and [K] intervened 'c'mon lad's cool it. [K] implied to Ferrit "I'll look into it".*

The letter indicates K standing as a powerful intermediary to be feared due to his own potential for violence, and the sprawling connections he had throughout the criminal underworld.[5] Yet, K demonstrates his ability as a level-headed negotiator in not only handling the phone call or organising the 'sit down', but also in defusing a potentially volatile situation in which both parties bore firearms. K's relationship with the Thompson crime family meant Arthur Junior could access contacts in Paisley to supply heroin. Yet he was unable to reap the financial rewards, being instead gunned down in 1991, by the suspected Paul Ferris (Ferris & McKay, 2001). Ferris suspected K as playing some role in aiding the Thompson family to reap revenge, with Ferris associates Bobby Glover, 31, and Joe Hanlon, 24, being assassinated in return (McKay, 2006). In the preceding years, it would be Jamie Daniel and Stuart 'Specky' Boyd that would benefit most from the supply routes forged – exploited for the distribution of the booming heroin trade of the late 80s and 1990s.

---

3 Indeed, Ferris had beaten a number of charges relating to attempted murder and one of murder.
4 The Ferrit is Brockwell's derogatory play on the name Ferris, indicating Paul Ferris.
5 Quotations from this letter are from an affidavit from an inmate associate with K. The letter is not available to the wider public.

THE SMACK TRADE ENTERS PAISLEY

Just as cannabis grew in popularity during 1960s Britain's countercultural movement, heroin exploded onto the scene in the late 1980s. In 1980, heroin use throughout Britain may have been as low as 10,000, yet by 1990, the number of users were counted in the hundreds of thousands. Addict typology and demographics had likewise changed during this time. Addicts no longer tended to be mid-to-older aged individuals, dispersed throughout the country, having become addicted to opioids through the ongoing treating of pain management, but rather addicts were now typically intravenous users, young men, from traditionally working-class backgrounds, and unemployed. A Home Office report (1998) indicates the 1980s heroin epidemic occurred in two distinct mini-waves. While somewhat localised parts of major cities, like London and Edinburgh, appear to follow Liverpool in having an outbreak in the early-mid-1980s, much of the remaining UK remained largely heroin-free until the second mini-wave in the early 1990s. In relation to drug use, and the aftermaths of ensuing violence and crime, in Paisley and the wider Renfrewshire area, show a steady increase in media and governmental reporting on the issue. As drug misuse increased in Paisley, so too did crime. Indeed, strong correlation exists between areas high in heroin addiction and crime (Casey et al., 2009). Yet what became unique was how criminal groups reorganised themselves around the trade to become highly specialised outfits.

The trafficking routes paved by K and a handful of others, created greater connectivity between underworld sources in Glasgow, predominantly the east end and northeast of the city, alongside Paisley. Although little more than 12 miles apart, in an era which lacked real instantaneous connectivity, either through the internet, motorway or public transport, and likewise in a region craved out by deeply ingrained territorialism and sectarianism, the city's East End could feel like a million miles away from Paisley's town centre.[6] This was especially so in the context of ongoing market-based underworld enterprises. Yet criminals like K, Thompson, Tam 'The Licensee' McGrew, Jamie 'The Bull' Stevenson and Stuart 'Specky' Boyd, among others, realised the importance of forging criminal networks across the region (Findlay, 2012a). K had been among the main players in Paisley at the time, but would subsequently be jailed in 1993. The void this created led to an eruption of violence in Paisley. Through his contacts in the East End of Glasgow, K had forged alliances with drug wholesaler Jamie Daniels. As K was known to be an important underworld figure in Paisley, Daniels was equally so in northeast Glasgow, in the Possilpark housing estate.

---

6 Indeed the M8 motorway was not completed until 1980.

Like many professional criminals of 1970s and 1980s Britain, Daniel primarily earned his living from predatory crimes like theft and robbery, usually of scrap metal (Findlay, 2012b). Recognising the growing hazards of predatory crime, both generally speaking and on a personal level following the death of his elder brother Robert from a theft gone wrong, Daniel would seek to take advance of the new era of global capitalism. He moved into market-based crime by muscling into the city's scrapyard industry in the 1980s. Yet the lure of a booming drugs trade would prove too much to resist for Daniel. The British Nationality Act (1948) had previously set in motion the economic and political conditions that saw a significant increase in immigration from former British colonies in the middle eastern into post-war Britain. Likewise, the subsequent Commonwealth Immigrants Act 1962 introduced the 'voucher system' that encouraged ethnic minorities to congregate in close kinship communities. While popular in major English cities like Birmingham, the same was not true to the same extent in Scotland where the congregation of immigrant populations was considerably less. Yet, some areas of Glasgow did undergo similar processes. The communities of Polloksheilds and Pollokshaws just south of the city centre became large settlements for middle eastern migrants.

Daniel exploited contacts in the criminal underworld to forge alliances with Asian smugglers in these communities (Findlay, 2012a). While the immigration of middle eastern populations into the United Kingdom increased criminal ability to access the trading routes to the poppy fields of Afghanistan, the ability to access high-grade heroin cheaply at the time had been aided by Russia's 1979 invasion of Afghanistan, resulting in resistance militia, the Mujahedeen, increasing opium production and sale, to fund weapons purchases. Indigenous criminals in the United Kingdom were increasingly aware of the potential having access to such networks would bring, and sought exploit connections. Daniel and an accomplice of Pakistan decent were imprisoned in 1983 for four and a half years for his part in trying to smuggle heroin into the country from Afghanistan via Heathrow Airport (Silvester, 2023).

Upon his release from prison, Daniels learnt from prior mistakes, and once again engaged in heroin smuggling with colleagues in Birmingham, via his Asian contacts in Glasgow. Having already gained a significant criminal reputation prior to drug smuggling, the Daniels crime family, now had steady finances to back this power up. The Daniels crime family, headed by Jamie, would dominate the underworld landscape in the city's northeast housing scheme, Possilpark. This dominance did not go unchallenged. In a criminal underworld where respect and violence go hand in hand, challengers always exist. Overcoming one of these challenges though brought particular kudos to the Daniels.

Frank McPhie, of Irish extraction, had gained a fearsome reputation in Glasgow's underworld as an armed robbery, illegal dog fighter and local hard men. McPhie likewise had been tied to several murders, including that of cellmate William Toye and former best friend Chris McGrory (Findlay, 2012a). On both occasion McPhie was given a not proven verdict. McPhie made early efforts like K in Paisley, and Jamie Daniels in Possilpark, to enter the burgeoning drugs trade. Like Jamie Daniels, McPhie was concerned with the heroin market giving its expedited growth. McPhie, like Jamie, was incarcerated, an eight-year prison sentence, for peddling drugs. Yet upon his release in 1998, McPhie would borrow Irish Republican Amry (IRA) money in an effort to get his foot back into the drugs trade. In the process though McPhie had a series of tit-for-tat disputes with several Daniels family members, on one occasion resulting in Jamie's nephew, Robert, being stabbed several times. While Findlay reports the dispute to have centred on dog fighting, it had possible undertones of McPhie trying to muscle in on the heroin trade in the city's Northeast. It was not long before McPhie and Jamie would exchange words with one another. During a brief meet on the street, McPhie though was in no mood to back down and threatened the lives of several Daniels family members. This prompted Daniels to act. Several weeks later, on 10 May 2000, McPhie was shot through the head from a sniper bullet, while entering his flat in Maryhill, near Possilpark. John McCabe, Jamie's right-hand man, was arrested, and later released, following lack of evidence, for the murder, yet investigative journalist Russel Findlay reported underworld grumbling that Daniels facilitated the murder in collusion with the IRA, given McPhie still owed considerable debt to the organisation. The murder of McPhie left a void in the Maryhill drugs trade, which Daniels would soon filled.[7]

Almost a decade prior to these events, Jamie Daniel had been trying to extend his business venture in the burgeoning heroin trade by looking to act as a wholesaler for other criminal groups across the West of Scotland, keen to bring heroin into their own territories. Ever the entrepreneur, Daniel intended to provide stable supply lines, and only required contacts to help connect him to interested parties. In Paisley, this was K. K had grown up in a particularly difficult period in the history of the community. Ferguslie Park had been considerably developed since the 1950s, owing to the Housing Act (1949), to become a large working-class community of 10,000 or so, living in dwellings which comprising 'four in a block' cottages as well as three and four story post-war tenements. The estate was hit hard by deindustrialisation, with closure of the huge Chrysler car plant in neighbouring Linwood, the nearby Stobo carpet factory and the textiles trade in the Ferguslie Mills.

---

7 The adjacent estate to the Daniel stronghold of Possilpark.

This resulted in fluctuating levels of unemployment among the population of Ferguslie Park, anywhere between 60–80%, during the period (Wright, 2018). Coupled with the heroin trade, drugs became the new commodity on the estate. Resultingly, K's generation proved particularly embedded in drug use and drug distribution. Given their significant access to firearms, some of K's peers where dangerous individuals. This generation included siblings Stuart and William 'Billy' Gillespie, Robert 'Piggy' Pickett, William 'Basil' Burns and his brother Roy and the McLaughlin brothers. In 1990, Daniel purchased a house in Linwood, the neighbouring estate to Ferguslie Park, and used his newly formed contacts to create supply lines trafficking heroin into the community. Yet he would not be the only one to do so, as George 'Goofy' Docherty, originating from Glasgow's East End, and Stuart Boyd, from the small town of Barrhead situated between Paisley and South Glasgow, whom he shared extended kinship with, befriended the Gillespie bothers and also sought to open up a supply route. K had shared prison time with Docherty and knew Boyd well, first from socialising in Paisley, and later having supplied him a steady flow of cannabis and amphetamines. K thus acted as an intermediary in keeping a potentially volatile environment, peaceful. However, this would change in 1992 when he was arrested for, and subsequently imprisoned formally in 1993, for drug trafficking (Ferris & McKay, 2001). This set the scene for a bloody feud which would refine the groups involved, propelling them to further specialisation in the drugs trade.

REORGANISING A CRIMINAL ORGANISATION

A counter cultural revolution in heroin misuse, combined with a national economic downturn, created ideal criminogenic conditions, does not of itself explain Paisley's 1990s inter-criminal group violence, nor the specialisation of remaining groups in the drugs trade. Nor does it explain why this specialisation then became the norm in Scotland. Political input, mismanagement and corruption were important additional ingredients. Indeed, the same would prove true just over a decade later in the north side of the city, helping fan the flames between the Daniels and Lyons crime families. The economic recession created by deindustrialisation particularly affected the disproportionately working-class population across the west of Scotland, including the town of Paisley. Ferguslie Park was hit hard and had significantly high rates of unemployment by 1980 (Collins, 1999). The quality of housing in the area itself, like so many post-war developments built rapidly using cheap materials, had fallen into a state of disrepair.

In addition, the Thatcher government's Housing Act (1980) introduced the Right to Buy Scheme. This Scheme allowed council house owners to purchase their homes for outright ownership. As such, those who owned homes in affluent sought-after areas purchased their homes, even if not initially, often over time, while the less desirable stock in poorer areas remained for social tenants. These destitute areas would became concentrated areas for the poor and the vulnerable. Estates like Ferguslie Park, comprising of mostly undesirable stock, quickly became identified as problem areas. Those who could leave often did, while the vacant housing stock was rented out cheaply to poor or 'problematic' tenants. New Public Management initiatives, and budgeting, also introduced by Thatcher's Conservative government, resulted in tighter constraints for housing upkeep, encouraging poor quality stock to remain open for rent, to avoid fines and fees (Ferlie, 2017).

Recognising the problem contributing factors were having in fuelling, what Wacquant terms, the *ghettoization* process, Westminster introduced large-scale urban regeneration funding. On 28 March 1988, Secretary of State for Scotland Malcolm Rifkind, likewise announced at parliament Scotland's own urban policy document, titled *New Life for Urban Scotland*, setting out ambitious plans to recreate Scotland's urban landscape. The urban regeneration strategy had been influenced by Wilson and Kelling's 'broken window' thesis (cited in Wilson & Hernstein, 1985). The thesis stated unkempt social housing would eventually result in minor delinquency via vandalism, which in turn would give rise to criminality. A 'run down' estate, would become a 'bad' estate conducive to criminogenic factors. While Wilson and Kelling's ideas, alongside Wacquant (2010) *ghettoization,* proved particularly impactful on policing and housing development in 1980s America, the narratives, while accepted in British circles, where nonetheless less stringently implemented. Economists Dean and Platt (2016), alongside criminologist John Pitts (2008), reviewed the Thatcher governments' housing policy. They suggest policy and initiatives which sought to boost the economy financially had the effect of creating slums, into which poor, reordered and often young families, including single parent households, were homed next to criminogenic populations and addicts. Consequently, instead of being aided and recognised as particularly vulnerable to economic and political conditions, such populations instead became an easy scapegoat for societal ills and poor policy decisions. Political influencers of the period, like Charles Murray (1984), offered favourable narratives that appealed to conservative policy-makers, stigmatising single parent households and young mothers for rearing feral children and blaming them for communal ills.

As part of Scotland's urban policy, in the 1980s, local authorities were assigned pre-agreed budgets, allotted by central government, to regenerate the most deprived communities. In Paisley, this meant Ferguslie Park. The urban renewal policy had a dual approach of first providing modern housing to tackle poverty, improve living standards and reduce the likelihood of crime. The policy also sought to regenerate employment in the area by implementing work incentives. Local Member of Parliament (MP) at the time jumped on the political bandwagon and announced the policy would renew the face of Ferguslie Park (Collins, 1999). In 1987, following support from then local Labour MP, Tommy Graham, alongside several other senior local Labour figures, the Ferguslie Park Community Business (FCB) initiative was established using a start-up fund of almost £200,000 of public money (BBC News, 1997). The FCB initiative was meant to be a community organisation funded by local government to bring employment to the area. Thus, Renfrewshire (from 1975 to 1996 Renfrew District Council under the umbrella of the vast Strathclyde Regional Council, when it was reorganised on a unitary basis as Renfrewshire Council) council was encouraged to award employment and work contracts to local residents of Ferguslie Park who wished to start their own businesses. It was thought at the time that the new Ferguslie Park should be designed for 'Fegs' by 'Fegs', whom were to be involved at all levels and in all spheres.[8] In reality, however FCB would award contracts to local criminals via associations and kinship within Renfrew District and later Renfrewshire council. One of these individuals was Billy Gillespie, who wished to start a security firm. His firm was contracted to ensure would-be thieves did not steal building materials, delivered regularly and left on site overnight, in the estates as the local authority authorised the demolishing of old housing stock, to be replaced with new modern accommodation. As part of the contract, Billy was encouraged to employ local residents as security guards; he inevitably turned to his brother, Stuart, and friends Pickett and, later, Docherty.

The FCB spawned organisation FCB Security was now essentially a legitimate organisation employing local criminals, paid for by taxpayers' money, to patrol and guard the community in which they tended to generate a great deal of fear and terror. Stuart Gillespie was then a feared loan shark, while Pickett was a violent individual who would go on to became probably the most feared gangster ever to walk the streets of Paisley. Similar urban renewal initiatives encouraged other criminals from around Glasgow and the west to start their own organisations, in unregulated areas like security and taxi firms. This move allowed professional criminal to move further away from predatory organised crime, towards more market-based activities. Advances in technology, communication, business, transport and international networking combined to accelerate the process (Barnes et al., 2011). Other criminals capitalising on

---

8 Feg is a local term used to describe a resident of Ferguslie Park.

these ventures, included Tam 'The Licensee' McGraw, TC Campbell, John Healy and Stevie Malcolm (Rannoc, 2019). The move into the security businesses would see FCB Security form a close, albeit unofficial alliance, with Stuart Boyd. Boyd had moved into the world of drug distribution and would become a steady supplier to Gillespie who was looking to do likewise. By 1990, the trafficking supply routes for the movement of cannabis, amphetamine and now heroin were up and running.

CHAPTER SUMMARY

While FCB proved useful in assisting the Gillespie brothers in laundering drug money, it is unlikely that the security firm was started up for this reason solely, as Teddy Rannoc (2019), a former criminal employed by Tam McGrew in the ice cream wars, notes. The rise of business enterprise in highly unregulated markets enabled criminals to deploy their key resource – violence. By drawing, almost literally in this context, on violence capital, they were able to muscle into the trade and provide a steady income for themselves. In some cases, where violence could be deployed regularly, they could monopolise the trade altogether. Money laundering was of some benefit to hiding drug money, but tapping into taxpayer funds and working jobs in the side, such as stealing, or arranging for the theft of goods from site, provided bigger incomes, at least initially.

This changed as the heroin trade expanded. Entry into the security trade would have been seen as a business venture in its own right. Stuart Gillespie had already acquired a significant 'hard-man' reputation in the area from both his earlier years as a street gang member of the local Young Team and his early adult years forged as a local no nonsense loan shark (Deuchar, 2013). Having also been raised in the area and growing up with other local gang members meant he had further muscle to draw upon in the persons of Pickett, Burns and Docherty. Backing from the local council, access to public funds, and corruption within the local authority, were the political factors needed to complement the cultural and economic factors already in place which shaped FCB Security into a vehicle for drug distribution. All it now required was a spark to set the whole process off. This was duly provided in 1995 – the beginning of the town's drug war.

5

THE 1995–1998 DRUG WARS

CHAPTER INTRODUCTION

The previous chapter examined emergence of a Scottish trafficker class, focusing on key actors such as K, Daniel and Stevenson. It traced how their enterprises supplied a series of professional criminal gangs which had prior operations and infrastructure in acts such as robbery, theft and security operations, among others, before they took advantage of the value in growing drug markets. This brought a change in their behaviour to reorganise specifically around drug supply. This chapter explores this aspect of gang reorganisation more specifically, by analysing the Paisley Drug Wars.

THE SPARK

The awarding of a council contract to Ferguslie Park Community Business (FCB) Security, spearheaded under the Scottish urban policy initiative, enabled criminal entrepreneur Billy Gillespie to head a security firm paid for by the taxpayer. The initiative encouraged preferential treatment from the council, giving further leverage. In reality Billy's elder brother, Stuart, unofficially headed the firm, but had been unable to himself own the company given an extensive criminal record. However, as seen here, bypassing legislation intended to keep criminals out of business enterprise and ownership is easily achieved. Billy, under Stuart's guidance, was able to exploit this preferential treatment and employ criminal peers to work as security guards on the estate. The contract was awarded on the premise that FCB oversee the security operation of the then newly developed housing stock and related building materials, in Ferguslie Park. FCB were initially opportunistic criminals. This began by providing themselves with a steady, and much inflated, wage. After some time, the group would use their position to employ 'ghost employees'. Ghosts never actually worked for the firm. While some of this income went to these ghosts, often real people on the estate, the bulk of wages went into the Gillespies' hands. A single 2014 interview carried out between the researcher and pseudonymised interviewee 'Andrew', as part of a University of the West of Scotland doctorate, illustrates the opportunistic, and somewhat simplistic, nature of initial ventures:

> *I*: What did [Stuart Gillespie] propose to you when meeting?
>
> *A*: I caught up with him on Barrochan (street)… he was saying I owed him, I owed him.
>
> *I*: Did you owe?
>
> *A*: I did owe but it was £20, nothing…. He said more. Way more… [but proposed] it (drug debt) be wiped if I said I worked for [FCB Security].
>
> *I*: Entailing what, here?
>
> *A*: I was to give my details… [he] would stick me on their books and pay me for it…. Like a small [sum]. I didn't want [to, but] I was getting money [from the welfare state] and couldn't….[Stuarts colleague] asked if I would hold some tools instead.[1]

While Andrew did not accept Gillespie's offer, nor was he aware of the exact mechanics involved, he was nonetheless aware that it involved fraudulent activity. After declining Andrew was subsequently offered the proposal to hold onto 'tools' – again the precise meaning of the term is not elaborated – as a way to clear debt. Andrew again declined. Andrew notes, Stuart inflated the debt owed in an effort to exert pressure, and thus control. This coercive control is a sustained feature of the illicit drugs trade. FCB would use money gained from ghosts – exploiting other preferential grants – and from organising the theft of building material from their own sites to resell; as a means to purchase heroin at wholesale level. The council contract also enabled the firm to rent industrial premises adjacent to the estate, as a base of operations. The rent on these premises was never actually paid, as the police investigation uncovered (The Herald, 1996a). Ventures were opportunistic and ad hoc. Organisation only

---

1 The colleague in question was unknown to participant Andrew, but spoke during his interaction with the pair.

really began when drugs were purchased at wholesale level from supplier Stuart Boyd – a contact brought about by extended kinship with Docherty.

The conditions needed for specialisation in drug distribution were in place. The final ingredient needed to begin this process of specialisation of Scottish criminal groups in drug distribution was a drug war. This occurred when converging factors ignited the required spark. Given K's remand and subsequent incarceration, a void in the cannabis and amphetamine market grew. In addition, a series of heroin shortages resulted in addicts using Temazepam substitutes. The prescription drug could be both consumed or dissolved and injected intravenously to alleviate opioid addiction. Oral consumption of Temazepam grew in popularity among the new 1990s recreational young drug users, as described by Parker and colleagues in their drug normalisation thesis (Parker et al., 1998). Converging factors created a demand for Temazepam. It was cheap, affordable, used across various drug users and above all profitable to sell. Gillespie, ever opportunistic, had been using FCB as an increasingly well-organised front for moving heroin around Ferguslie. Contractual agreements allowed FCB to make a visible presence in the public domain, ostensibly as a deterrence against theft. FCB though used this perversely to ensure drugs were sold openly from a series of dedicated tenement buildings, typically located around the now demolished shops at the end of Ferguslie Park Avenue. The area became known locally as 'Fort Apache'.

Under FCB's gaze, the tenements were used by dealers to take customers' orders. The dealers would then pass the order to a runner inside the building, who would make a collection from any one of six homes within the building. This made gathering evidence by police, or potential theft by would-be robbers, very difficult. FCB would ensure supply was regular, while any police presence was identified immediately. Outsiders would be questioned, and muscle was on hand if needed. It should be noted that, while still unproven, it was suspected that police corruption was rife as the time, with FCB Security having several officers on their payroll. Gillespie now saw an opportunity to ensure complete dominance over the estate. With K in prison and FCB as the main supplier of drugs, Gillespie decided to move to monopolise the trade completely. Gary, a key actor in the drugs war during this period, explains:

> *Only a couple of people know why the drug war started... Round about [19]93, or 94... Stuart said [FCB Security] ran [Ferguslie Park]... decid[ing] everyone had to buy... drugs from him. You wanted heroin or jellies, you buy from him. If you were a dealer, you [knew where to get] drugs [to sell] from Stuart.... Loads [of] people selling their own merchandise... [but] Stuart tried to stop that. He [succeeded] for [some time]. Stopp[ing] everyone in Feegie... [and] the West End, Top-End of Foxbar, selling...*

> *unless they bought from him...a lot of hard cunts about [however]. Johnny McLaughlin in Linwood, Cochran's in Foxbar... they [rebelled]... Stuart couldn't stop them selling... Johnny [McLaughlin] and Sloan decided to get [Stuart] to pull his head back in and shot his house up... [They] shot Stuart's neighbours house by mistake. A guy might have died or got paralysed.... Johnny was going to shot Stuart's house, as a warning, you know, no[t] to kill him, but warn him... [Johnny and Stuart] didn't always see things [eye to eye] but they [were amicable] before the [incident]... Johnny dealt [heroin and] jellies.*

As a veteran and active player of the drugs war, Gary states the reasons for the drugs war had previously been known to only a handful of people. The statement given by Gary is supported by a media report on the shooting of an innocent man, Gordon Petrie, at his house on Glencoats Drive, Ferguslie Park, in January 1995. He was shot through the back while watching television (*The Herald*, 1996b). Mr Petrie was indeed Stuart Gillespie's neighbour at the time.

THE RISE OF GUN VIOLENCE IN PAISLEY

While Mr Petrie's shooting indicated to Stuart Gillespie that he was the likely intended target, this was possible mainly due to the prevalence of firearms of the streets of mid-1990s Paisley. The availability of readily accessible firearms and ammunition played a significant role in the growth of the drug war. Lax laws on firearms in the immediate post-war period meant many criminals had access to guns. Firearms proved a useful commodity for carrying out predatory crimes like armed robbery. Yet during robbery, firearms were typically presented as a method of intimidation, thus rarely used. Likewise initial market-based criminals muscling into unregulated areas of commerce had little use for firearms except as threats. The drugs trade was different in that it pitted criminals against criminals, with neither likely to back down. Participant Gordo, interviewed as part of a 2018 study into firearm prevalence, carried out by the researcher and colleagues, states:

> *Guns weren't rare [in 1960]. My dad had one. Everybody had [one or knew] someone who did... My dad and his [friends] hunt[ed] the rabbits up the fields... the Parish paid him to keep rabbits off their land.... People weren't shooting people.... laws changed [after] Dunblane [the 1996 school mass shooting, discussed below]... and [subsequent guns amnesties]... [which saw many] people give [their firearms] up... Even though people had guns, it was like*

> *having knives. Sometimes they got used... but not really. The community was good when I was young. You [c]ould leave your doors open... [sure the tenement] had to be clean or... you could get evicted... drugs changed [this consensus]. You had idiots, high on drugs, fighting, shooting... The younger ones were all into taking junk, arguing, going home, getting a gun and shooting. Then the guy that's been shot at, is out his face, no[t] caring, retaliates.* Gordo

Gordo, then 60, recalled his childhood years as being relatively drug-free. Post-war Ferguslie Park had strong intergenerational ties. Relatedly, the awareness that others may have had access to firearms resulted in mutual respect for potential violence capital. Disputes rarely led to firearms incidents in practice. Yet by the 1990s, the criminal landscape in Ferguslie Park had changed. The introduction of heroin, the congregation of poor, marginalised and 'problem' populations in residualised housing stock, saw community bonds gradually erode. Individuals were more inclined to react violently given that they tended to lack ties to the wider community. Drug addiction could further inhibit their self-restraint. Those with firearms were cognisant that less people had access following changes to the law, and thus could use their monopolisation of violence capabilities over others.

As Gordo notes, while a number of firearm laws sought to reduce and instil greater control, the Dunblane massacre brought about an overhaul in the United Kingdom, and more specifically, Scotland's, gun laws. During the early weekday morning of 13th March 1996, Thomas Hamilton walked into Dunblane Primary School, Perthshire, armed with four legally held handguns, two 9 mm Browning HP pistols, two Smith & Wesson M19 .357 Magnum revolvers and 743 ammunition cartridges. After entering the school gymnasium, Hamilton encountered 28 Primary one pupils and three members of staff, who were preparing for a PE lesson. Hamilton opened fire and shot dead 16 pupils and one teacher, and injured a further 15, before killing himself (Cullen, 1996). The incident was met with public outrage and stirred debate regarding gun laws in Britain (Squires, 2000). The subsequent Cullen Report, in 1996, alongside a public led campaign, known as the Snowdrop Campaign, introduced legislation, specifically two new Firearms Acts, outlawing private ownership of most handguns. The UK Government's 1996 buy back initiative likewise helped remove many existing guns from the streets. It is noteworthy, if beyond this book's specific focus, that buy back initiatives and associated legislation have been relatively successful in the UK context, which, distinct from the United States, has no constitutional equivalent to the second amendment and its 'right to bear arms' affirmed by Supreme Court jurisprudence such as in *District of Columbia v Heller* (United States Supreme Court, 2008). The rates of gun ownership (3.3 per 100 people in the United Kingdom – encompassing Scotland, England and Wales but excluding Northern Ireland, compared to 101 per 100 people in the United States) and annual rates of gun homicide (0.03 per 100,000 in the United Kingdom compared to 3.6 per 100,000 in the United States) further indicate profoundly different gun cultures interlaced with divergent constitutional regimes between the two nations (Gun Control Network, 2024). The UK's post-Dunblane initiatives are largely credited with bringing about more restrictive gun laws, and credited with taking tens of thousands of illegal or unwanted firearms off the streets (Squires et al., 2008).

These laws though would unfortunately come too late for much of the drug war, but undoubtedly helped stifle its escalation. FCB Security however had already had a history of using firearms to intimidate and threaten. Indeed, Pickett was charged with intimidation of local political figures, while Gillespie placed a £10,000 contract on the head of then Labour MP for Paisley North, Irene Adams, for speaking out against council corruption (Panorama, 1996). FCB Security would use rented premises to store and stockpile firearms, and later drugs. The motive here was not so much the stricter gun laws as removing a number of potential weapons from being used against them. This tactic that had some value given gun laws and amnesties after 1996 reduced significantly the amount of weapons on the streets. Yet, the criminal group had ties to Boyd, whose driver John 'Joker' McCartney, was a member of a (still legal) gun club, and regularly used this membership to access ammunition (McKay, 2002). Ties to firearms in the criminal underworld became more valuable with drug profitability, gun restrictions and the closure of many hunting shops which also specialised in firearms such as Pitcher Sports, on the Paisley High Street.

CHALLENGES, CHALLENGERS AND ALLIANCES

In the years leading up to the drug war in 1995, FCB Security had established themselves as the main criminal organisation in Paisley. Stuart Boyd had been setting up a parallel organisation on Glasgow's south side. Boyd grew up between Priesthill in south Glasgow, and, Barrhead, a neighbouring suburb situated between Glasgow and Paisley. In his younger years, Boyd, like K, had forged a formidable criminal reputation with local street gangs. He would draw upon these peer networks to form a criminal group in adulthood. Boyd's criminal group operated out of the Royal Oak pub in Nitshill, and from there arranged shipments of heroin, cannabis and amphetamines from Liverpool and Manchester, to distribute across south Glasgow, Barrhead and Paisley. It was through these networks, and socialising in Paisley's then busting nightlife, that Boyd formed a close alliance with Gillespie. His extended kinship with Docherty, and Docherty's subsequent relationship with one of the FCB member's sister, aided his progress. Boyd supplied Gillespie with drugs to distribute in Ferguslie Park.

Like Ferguslie Park's, the landscape of Barrhead and South Glasgow had changed considerably since the post-war period, deindustrialisation and urban regeneration. During this time local professional criminals had, as in Paisley, begun to move away from predatory crimes in the post-war period, towards market-based crimes by the 1960/1970s, before beginning to get involved in the growing drugs trade. This first involved cannabis and later heroin and pills, with criminal groups acting either as distributors, muscle for hire or robbers. Yet, unlike conditions in Ferguslie Park, these communities, like the west of Scotland as a whole, lacked the political intervention that legitimised the criminal behaviour of FCB Security, as drug distributers, in the eyes of many local politicians, authority figures and the public. While criminals and criminal groups in Glasgow engaged in drug distribution, and some rose to considerable positions of power, none operated quite like FCB Security, making effort to completely monopolise the drug trade in terms of provision and service over particular geographical localities. FCB Security were not only breaking the law, but doing so in a very visible manner, and with local political backing. This made FCB Security unique at the time.

Boyd's criminal group was certainly one of those criminal outfits operating at the higher echelons of the drug trade in south Glasgow in the early 1990s. Yet Boyd's burgeoning alliance with Gillespie would inevitably see him became embroiled in the emerging Paisley feud. Interviewee Gary had been an associate of Boyd, during the 1990s.

> *Boyd was dangerous... Not to be messed with. I liked him, we got on. [We] did some work. He was getting some shit from his usual supplier... he had two really, and I helped him out... [I] never got in his pocket but... Him and Stuart [Gillespie] were close. Boyd sold [heroin] to Stuart. Stuart [Gillespie] had his own firm but.... [he] ran his own mob. He was skinny but... A wee pitbull... Boyd was more, well a guy you might struggle to read. He would laugh wi[th] you, but you never second guessed him... He was paranoid.*

> *If you worked wi[th] him, you ended up dead. He [got] paranoid and [had] his own guys killed... Police reckon [Boyd] was responsible for... about ten killings. It was never about drugs... the killings Boyd [arranged] was [his] paranoia... he had two main boys that done his dirty work, one [he] killed. Gary*

Gary's statement although not exclusively saying so, makes reference to Boyd's younger cousin John Simpson as having been one of the enforcers he had killed. Gary, having worked with Boyd, and a number of Boyd's associates, shed some insight into his personality and state of mind in regard to his role in criminal ventures. Gary presents Boyd as a likeable, clever and intelligent individual who was nonetheless acutely paranoid. This image is supported by autobiographical accounts, including Reg McKay publication, *Armed Candy* (2002), regarding Boyd's former girlfriend.

FCB Security sought to wholly monopolise the drug trade in Ferguslie Park, and Boyd's criminal group operated among the few at the higher echelons of drug supply in South Glasgow. But as noted from the attempted shooting of Gillespie in 1995, criminal groups were by no means shy of challengers. Participant Gary notes 'The McLaughlin', 'Cochran's' and 'Winter's [crime families]', all proved challengers. While Boyd sold drugs to FCB Security, Jamie Daniel would sell drugs to Gillespie's rivals, i.e. Johnny McLaughlin, who forged a strong association with the Cochran brothers. In 1993, K's incarceration and left his role as a de facto peacekeeping intermediary in abeyance. Into this void, separate supply lines emerged to facilitate the movement of not only heroin but also cannabis, cocaine and amphetamines. Between 1990 and 1994 the growing drug trade and the efforts to monopolise that trade saw a steady rise of violence in Renfrewshire county more widely. While this violence tended to concentrate on Ferguslie Park, the wider town, suburbs and South Glasgow were pulled in. A fall-out between former friends Robert Pickett and Billy Gillespie on one side, and the Cochran brothers – Stephen, Brian, Hugh and Robert – on the other, over an outstanding drug debt, in 1990, set the trend for an ongoing feud that would run until the conclusion of the drug war. In March 1990, three of the Cochran brothers, Brian, Stephen and Robert, were arrested and charged with the shooting of Billy Gillespie and attempted murder of Pickett (The Herald, 1995a). Following the shooting, Billy and Pickett engaged in a spate of tit-for-tat incidents, including Pickett slashing brother Hugh across the face and neck outside the St Mirren (football) Club in Paisley, following his attendance at a funeral. In response, Brian and Robert Cochran conspired to murder Pickett, and armed with shotguns, parked their vehicle on Ferguslie Park Avenue waiting to ambush Pickett. Yet while lying in wait, Pickett had been tipped off concerning their presence and would approach the parked car from a concealed position. Armed with a handgun, Pickett would discharge the firearm into the car. Brian Cochrane suffered serious injury to the chest, abdomen and back, while Robert had three bullet fragments removed from in his head (*The Herald*, 1995a).

A year later, in 1991, three shootings occurred within a week, marking a significant heightening of tension. The first incident, saw a local man aligned to Gillespie group shot in his own flat in the town centre. The second incident involved a gunman, believed to be one of the Winters brothers from the adjacent town of Johnstone, try and gain entry to the Cochran family home in Oliphant crescent, Foxbar, before discharging a firearm, striking Brain Cochran in the face. Although wounded he survived. The Cochrans responded in kind by stabbing out the eye of one of the Winters brothers. The third incident in the week was as equally brazen. Two men sat inside a red Montego, parked outside the town's Sheriff court in broad daylight. Following the arrival for their court appearance over the shooting of Billy Gillespie, the Cochran brothers would park outside the court in brother Hugh's Ford Escort. Before exiting the vehicle, the duo in the red Montego would start the car engine, swing across the road, leaning out the car window on the passenger side, firing several shots from a handgun through the Escort's window. One of the bullets would hit Robert Cochran in stomach, while another missed completely and instead went through the window of the court itself. The Montego would later be found burned out in a field outside of Paisley. The pair were never identified, but were believed to have been Pickett and William Burns. Tensions increased and in 1993, Michael Quigg, a Pickett associate, murdered a Cochran associate, Michael Holmes (The Herald, 1993c).

While the spate of violence around the drug trade saw a number of incidents ensue which engrained bad blood between all parties in Paisley, in Glasgow/Barrhead Boyd had also been involved in organising his own criminal group around his leadership. This included recruiting William Burns, whom Boyd had also befriended from Basil's time living in social housing in a since-demolished Barrhead tower block, to shot 23-year-old Raymond McCafferty (The Herald, 1994a). Burns had steadily been gaining a reputation as a gun for hire (Findlay, 2018). It is believed Boyd used the services of Burns, and his associate from Neilston (a small village attached to Barrhead) Joe 'Vino' Finnegan, to shoot McCafferty of Roukenburn Street, Pollok, in February 1994. McCafferty was shot and killed by the pair as he left his home and crossed the nearby carpark. However, Finnegan would be acquitted, while Burns was found not guilty due to insufficient evidence. Burns would however be in trouble again in November 1994 after he stole a birthday cake from Marks & Spencer supermarket in Paisley centre, during which a security guard Alan Morrison challenged him (Daily Record, 1996). Basil responded by brandishing a 9 mm Browning automatic handgun in Mr Morrison's face and threatening to kill him. Basil made bail but was later jailed for six years. Boyd is also thought to be responsible for the killing of Barrhead man David McGaughey, 29, of Bowerwalls Street (The Herald, 1994b). McGaughey had been involved in a spate of violent incidents with Boyd regarding drug debts He was found shot dead on 16 March 1994, in Commercial Lane (off Commercial Road in the Waulkmill area of Barrhead) after leaving for his work at about 6.30 a.m. on Monday. He had been stabbed repeatedly with a knife, shot several times with a small-calibre handgun and partly set on fire with a flammable liquid such as petrol. Detective Superintendent Bill Gordon, one of the officers leading the investigation, said he believed the murderer or murderers, to have lived locally. Boyd indeed lived less than a mile away from the scene.

The incidents likewise entrenched each group into their own well-defined sides. Using their own suppliers, and distributing to their own set of customers, as well as many also using drugs themselves, meant the set boundaries and bad blood helped organise the criminal groups. The efforts of FCB Security to then attempt to monopolise control through a power grab made war inevitable.

WAR YEARS: 1995–1998

Although shootings and stabbings had become an almost weekly occurrence over the three years prior to the targeting of Gillespie at his home in 1995, fortunately few had been killed. However, this would change drastically in 1995 and the following three years. The year 1995 saw intensified violence in the Paisley drug war (PDW) as several murders unfolded. Gillespie's efforts to monopolise the drug trade, and his attempted assassination, led to a series of ad hoc and reactive events. These engulfed the town in a drug war to ensure dominance and control of the burgeoning drugs trade. Recognising the growing pattern of violence and corruption with FCB initiatives, police Scotland implemented Operation Dragon, with objectives to reduce firearm and drug-related violence in Paisley (The Herald, 1995c). Following the attempted assassination of Gillespie in January 1995, FCB responded in anger. Having been given information that McLaughlin was responsible, Gillespie tried to have him killed. The resulting tension between McLaughlin and Gillespie saw

Johnny McLaughlin go on the offencive. Along with associate Gerard McTavish, the pair made a desperate effort to hunt down and assassinate Gillespie and his associates. One associate was John 'Dip' Kelly. On Sunday 12 March 1995, McLaughlin and McTavish used a stolen car to visit known haunts in which Dip drank (The Herald, 1995d). Entering the Caledonia Bar in Shortroods, the pair dragged a friend of Dip, Mr John 'Jocky' Kennedy, from the pub in broad daylight. Bundling Mr Kennedy into the back of the stolen van, Johnny shot him in the leg to extract information as to Dip's whereabouts. The pair then drove to the Park Bar in Paisley's West End, entering the premises around 8 p.m. While McTavish pointing out Dip Kelly among the crowd, Johnny McLaughlin used a handgun to fire several shots in his direction. One shot struck Dip Kelly in the eye, to his permanent disfigurement. He survived the attack however, and would later be charged himself with permanently disfiguring a young man with a golf club.

Two days after the Park Bar shooting, Gillespie and co would retaliate by killing Johnny McLaughlin's brother, Drew McLaughlin (Panorama, 1996). While residing at his home along with his brother Mark, his wife and child, it is believed, given that the case is unsolved, that while on bail William Burns and George Docherty travelled to Andrew's home in the now demolished blocks of flats at Armour Place, Linwood. The taxi trade was still largely unregulated, and, as noted in the previous chapter, local drug dealers would use regular drivers to courier them to various locations. Using one such regular driver, two of Gillespie's men entered the taxi, which dropped the duo outside their destination. The pair entered the block of flats, which had an open communal door, making their way to Drew's front door. They knocked on the door, and on seeing his blurred figure through the stained glass panel, unleashed a barrage of shotgun pellets. The shots struck Drew's face and body, killing him (Panorama, 1996). The killers made haste, exiting the block and entering the nearby taxi to make their getaway. In that same week a young dealer Michael Docherty was also shot at his front door (The Herald, 1995e).

Later in March 1995, Gillespie asked Boyd for assistance in helping him bring Paisley's drug trade under his control. Given this aided Boyd's own revenue as Gillespie's main supplier, he agreed. Boyd lured Brian 'Doppy' Cochrane, aged 31, to his death by having him killed on his turf in Pollok (The Herald, 1995f). Doppy had proved an ample fighter, an astute dealer and a formidable opponent to Gillespie in hindering his control of Foxbar's drug market. Foxbar is the estate adjacent to Ferguslie Park. Reports indicate Doppy was lured to Pollok under a false pretence. The exact details however are missing. While sitting at the wheel of his parked vehicle on Glenora Drive, in Pollok, Glasgow, he was assassinated. To date the murder remains unsolved;

Gerald Egan, 24, from Barrhead, and Charles Melvin, 30, from Pollok, went on trial accused of his killing but the charges were not proven. Melvin though would later vanish in 2000 after a falling-out with Boyd (*Daily Record*, 2003). Melvin's wife, Margaret, believed Boyd ordered his abduction and murder following a disagreement. Ironically, only a few weeks before this series of incidents, Chief Constable Leslie Sharp of Strathclyde Police announced another set of improving figures, claiming violence had decreased by 10% in the Renfrewshire (K) Division, covering Paisley, Johnstone and Linwood (The Herald, 1995g). Herald reporter James Freeman however claimed the figures 'don't add up' with actual incidents and were presented to skew the loss of police control over the area – more so given the decline in reported violence is in those localities in which The Winters, McLaughlin and Cochran crime families, and FCB Security, operated. It is more likely the public simply do not report incidents, much of which occur in the underworld also. The summer months of 1995 saw a decline in reporting on key actors being targeted. Yet, despite the seriousness and frequency of violence in Paisley, it did not grab the media attention one might expect. The BBC though produced an episode, as part of its *Panorama* series, titled 'Drug Rule' covering the Paisley drug war.

Aired first on 24 July 1996, it opens with the admission of a young girl into the local Royal Alexandria Hospitals A&E department. Intoxicated from a concoction of alcohol and Temazepam abuse, the young girl requires to have her stomach pumped. The next scene is the admission of a young man with stab wounds, having also been slashed on the face. Mr Ken Mitchell, a surgeon at the Royal Alexandra Hospital in Paisley, told the programme, given the injuries of the patients he regularly treats 'There's obviously... some sort of warfare going on,' (*Panorama*, 1996) and recalls one recent victim having 'stab wounds through the neck, going in one side, out the other side, right through the vocal cord area'. The programme concludes with the subsequent murder of the man, filmed earlier in A&E. While the man was anonymised in the programme, his mother later came forward after the programme was aired, with an appeal for witnesses to come forward with any information regarding his murder. Although not naming those responsible, Mrs Greenlees suspected a family from the same estate, in Johnstone, to be responsible. Ironically, this is the same estate as the Winters crime family. Kenneth Greenlees of Dundonald Avenue, Johnstone, was just 24 when he was shot dead as he crossed the town's Thomas Shanks park on route to a local bar around 11 p.m., Saturday, 23 July (The Herald, 1995i).

Then in late autumn 1995, the PDW saw the entry of a new group of actors, the Rennie brothers. The brothers were known heroin users and dealers, and like other dealers on the Ferguslie Park estate had been ordered by Gillespie to pay a fee for the right to sell drugs. As with many others, Rennie refused to comply and would attack Billy Gillespie as well as smashing his motor vehicle in a public display to refusal. Then on the 2 November 1995, Billy's brother Stuart Gillespie, along with associates Piggy and Goofy, approached the Rennie family home armed, kitted in FCB outfits and armed with a handgun and machete (The Herald, 1996b). The brothers, Brian, Paul and Scott exited the family home along with a friend John Mullen, on Candren Road, Ferguslie Park, in order to confront the three visitors. It was at that point that a dispute ensued and Gillespie pointed at one of the elder brothers and told Pickett to 'shoot the fat bastard' (Findlay, 2012a); however the gun jammed and would not work. A brawl would break out, and a bloodbath would ensue given that Docherty armed with a machete wade in, assaulting several of the Rennie males. While the case went through the process of going to court, this only stifled incidents for a short period. The feud was far from finished. On 23 May 1996, the Rennie brothers retaliated by smashing the car window of Mr Gillespie's girlfriend, as it sat in his driveway at his home in Glencoats Drive. Upon inspecting the damage, Mark Rennie ambushed Billy and shot him in the chest with a shotgun (*The Herald*, 1996b). He survived. The following day, the Rennie brothers fired shots through the home window of Stuart Gillespie. The next day, 25 May 1996, Stuart Gillespie eventually shot and killed Mark Rennie. Mark had in the prior months begun dating Margaret Brown, 34. Margaret lived on Glencoats Drive. Mark used this as a vantage point for observing the movements, and staging attacks on, the Gillespie brothers. This put the individuals at even more odds with one another. Margaret Brown testified that on the day of her boyfriend's murder she saw a masked man aim a handgun at Mark, 27. He had left her premises to draw trouble away from his family home on Candren Road, following news of a disturbance. Rennie had armed himself with a double-barrelled, sawn-off shotgun, hidden in his jacket sleeve, but upon exiting Brown's home, he was approached from behind and shot. Several of Gillespie's criminal group went on trial for the murder, including Gillespie, Docherty, Pickett and Mr Robert Forbes, 28, and Mr Steven McNamara, 22.[2] As Mark lay dying, the men approached him, and stood over him, laughing as he died (The Herald, 1997). Although Stuart Gillespie was convicted of his murder, many suspected Stuart Boyd of being the real shooter. He fled to Spain, before being extradited back to face trial, leading to a not proven verdict. Boyd returned to the Costa Del Sol, Spain, but was killed in 2003 following a firebomb attack on his family car. In the blaze Boyd,

---

2 Forbes himself would later have a falling-out with Pickett and as a result would be stabbed several times by a relative of Pickett.

his partner and child, as well as her young female friend, perished. Their deaths were attributed to the Russian Mafia, over a drug deal gone wrong.

The intensification of fighting between the groups only served to refine them into well-drilled and cohesive outfits. Drugs were bought in bulk, supplied into Paisley through a few dedicated lines, except for prescription pills which were often stolen from raids on chemists, stolen prescriptions or secured from alternative sources. The arrangement of their sale was well organised and overseen by hierarchical processes, and anyone making effort to disrupt or muscle into the trade was deterred by violence. Yet, during 1995, K was freed from prison, and back on the streets. Local press sensationalised his release, touting Mr P would only add to the drug war. In response, on 2 June 1995, he fire-bombed the publishers. While Mr Alex Lumsden, managing director of Scottish and Universal Newspapers, claimed 'coverage of recent drug-related events in Paisley may have led to the attack on our premises', it was in fact due to a series of derogatory remarks made about close family members (The Herald, 1995h). In addition, K, being an astute intermediary, was able to begin to bridge some of the warring factions.

This was aided by the demise of FCB Security following the attempted murder of the Rennie brothers, and the eventual murder of Mark Rennie, along with a long running police investigation into political corruption and the mismanagement of funds. Billy Gillespie would later die from suicide. Likewise, at the same time, the McLaughlin and Cochran alliance was significantly weakened following the death of Brian Cochran, and long-term injuries on Robert having been shot on several occasions, as well as the incarceration of Johnny McLaughlin. This left a void into which K could step. K was able to forge a formidable crew, with Brockwell and David Donnell. Donnell, originally from Ferguslie Park, was a feared gunman, affiliated with the Winters in Johnstone, having beaten a murder rap alongside James Winter.[3] This helped smooth business relations. Donnell was jailed in 2000, following his efforts to have another Ferguslie Park drug dealer, Samuel Maxwell, murdered. Those hired to shoot Maxwell, killed innocent businessman, Billy Fargher, instead, due to misidentification. It is worth noting that several efforts would be made in subsequent years, by several actors, to assassinate Maxwell (The Herald, 2003).

---

3 James Winters was convicted in 2021 for a series of acts of sexual abuse against children (Paisley Daily Express, 2021).

The drugs war was still far from over and in 1997, another Ferguslie Park-based crime family, the Wingates, attempted to fill the void left by Gillespie. Brother David Wingate would get into a confrontation with a hardy individual from the Linwood area, Paul Hainey in November 1997 (*Daily Record, 1999*). It is unsure what the prior confrontation was about, as Hainey had loose links to drug dealing, but was known to be a user of Temazepam, but nonetheless was shot and killed by Wingate; however the case never went to trial. Wingate, along with two accused, Stephen Bryson and Richard Lewis (from Seedhill), were accused of murdering Hainey in the village of Houston. Paul Hainey, 21, a plumber, from Shortroods, was shot in the chest and back. However, David Wingate, would be killed little more than 12 months later, in December 1998, in what was believed to be a revenge attack. While out in the busy Shuttle Street area of Paisley town centre, Wingate was approached by an unknown individual outside Fury Murray's nightclub around 1 a.m., and blasted five times with a shotgun. As K's brother, had met Wingate while he was out, it was rumoured that K had been the shooter. However, this is possibly hearsay, and the case remains unsolved. Given the scope and word restriction of this book series, it is important to note that a number of other incidents occurred which simply cannot be covered here.

CHAPTER SUMMARY

It was estimated that during the period in which FCB had been in operation, at its height approximately £300,000 was being drained from taxpayers' money annually. Investigation into the accounting for missing money would prove inconclusive, but it was widely assumed that it had been filtered into the pockets of Gillespie, his colleagues and quite possibly a handful of those involved in local politics (McKay, 2002). While criminal groups across the west of Scotland began to reorganise around market-based organised crime in the form of drug distribution, it was local political corruption which enabled Gillespie's criminal group to begin to legitimise themselves, in the guise of FCB Security. The group's legitimation allowed them to gain local prestige as the main criminal outfit in the town, backed vocally by local politicians. Herein lies the problem. Being manager of the company and having access to funds and facilities, the group were able to use taxpayers' money to purchase drugs at wholesale level from Boyd. They then stored them in a number of local premises, as well as employing youths, drug users, local residents or indebted individuals through loan sharking, to sell drugs on an open market. Twenty four-hour surveillance and muscle could be provided by FCB employees such as Gillespie and Piggy. Officially speaking, given that large areas of housing in Ferguslie Park were undergoing regeneration or modernisation all at once, meant that FCB had to have a presence across much of the community to oversee the constant delivery of materials, and deter potential theft and vandalism. In addition, local shops and businesses could now also be extorted for protection money. The group gradually became specialised around drug distribution. Other criminal groups followed suit where possible. The added tension from outward and inward sources only served to further enhance gang ability to overcome obstacles and specialise in drug disruption solely. Yet, by 1997, though the plug had been pulled on FCB as a local MP Irene Adams spoke out against the corruption. Irene Adams herself had personally been victimised as she shared some degree of kinship with Gillespie associates, one of whom would steal her banking information to fund a local spending spree and holiday. Her speaking out resulted in a contract being taken out on her life.

6

HISTORY REPEATS ITSELF IN NORTH GLASGOW

CHAPTER INTRODUCTION

The previous chapters first of all traced how a trafficking class involved in the consistent supply of drugs emerged in the 1980s, and how this impacted upon existing criminal professional groups involved in various underworld activities such as illegal private hire taxis, security and robbery. Then they examined the criminal groups' reorganisation as they centred their activities on illegal drug supply. Together, these chapters indicated how political and economic changes from the 1970s onward contributed and strengthened criminal resolve to be involved in drug-related organised crime. This chapter builds on the prior discussion of related events in Paisley, showing how similar factors which occurred then repeated themselves in North Glasgow. This led to 'history repeating itself' in the form of a new drugs war between the Lyons and Daniels crime families. Unless otherwise indicated through references, the information about Eddie Lyons' activities in this chapter are derived from Findlay (2012a).

DANIELS V LYONS

While the drug war raged in Paisley, Glasgow had its own problems. However, although local criminal disputes frequently emerged, these tended to be concerned with challenges to one's status, disrespect, personal vendettas and even drug debts, among other issues. None of the disputes though had yet expanded to become outright wars seeking drug market monopolisation, and suppression of all others. Indeed, the late 1980s and early 1990s had seen a number of disputes envelop whole communities in tit-for-tat violence and killings, such as the ice cream wars (BBC iPlayer, 2023), Ferris v Thompson (Ferris & McKay, 2001), among others, but none were in specific relation to the control of drug markets.[1] Drug specialisation, until the mid-1990s, was largely reserved for those criminal groups to have emerged from the Paisley drug war (PDW). The political influence allotted to Ferguslie Park community business (FCB) Security undoubtedly changed the landscape as trade and service monopolisation occurred. Yet, similar patterns played out in the early 2000s, this time on Glasgow's North side. This involved drug trafficker and scrap metal thief, Jamie Daniels – briefly mentioned in prior chapters. His main antagonist in this emerging feud was Eddie Lyons Senior.

Unlike Jamie Daniel, Eddie Lyons Senior was an unlikely candidate to become one of Britain's most notable criminal figures. While Jamie Daniel was fearsome, relying on brute strength, Eddie Lyons had neither advantage. Rather investigative journalist Russell Findlay, who covered the feud extensively, described Eddie Lyons Senior as a 'busy body', and 'gossip', who befriended those in powerful positions in the underworld and legitimate society, including police and political figures. Yet, Lyons was cunning, and highly intelligent. Findlay describes him as possessing a unique ability to take 'snippets of information' from various sources and use it to his own advantage. Findlay provides the perfect example in his book *Caught in the Crossfire* (2012a) demonstrating how Eddie stirred trouble between two rivals to eliminate competition, allowing him to move into more serious forms of criminality. Prior to this, in the early 1990s, Eddie's criminal ventures had centred upon fraud, illegal piracy and selling stolen merchandise (often acquired from his brothers Johnny and Michael Lyons Senior, who were renowned-armed robbers). Like K in Paisley, Eddie used his interpersonal capabilities and contacts to form strong networks in which illegal products could be accessed and moved.

Findley details how Eddie had learned on 2 January 1984, aged 25, that he was no fighter himself, and that any criminal venture required a different methodology. Prior to this date Eddie had like other criminals tried to base his reputation on hyper-masculine attributes. Yet, while living at his parents' home, on Scapa Street, Cadder, along with his wife Josephine and their three sons, Eddie Junior (4), Stephen (3) and new-born Garry, members of the Moran crime family broke into the house and Robert 'Barra' Moran stabbed Eddie in the chest. Eddie survived, and testified at the subsequent trial, giving evidence against Barra, who received a three year prison sentence. However, according to Findlay (2012),

---

1 Note, the ice cream wars had nothing to do with drugs, despite media speculation and dramatisation, as noted by several insiders such as Paul Ferris, TC Campbell and Teddy Rannoc.

Eddie was labelled a 'grass' and forced to move to the new built estate of Milton only several miles across the city. While only a few miles away, the relocation helped defuse the situation. Eddie Senior struggled to shake off negative labelling but could use this to his advantage and instead formed close ties to police, and politicians, alike. They proved useful allies. Eddie's wider family relocated to Milton over time. While Milton bordered Possilpark, it was perceived as a largely middle-class estate, with a leafy landscape, and a mixture of owner occupiers and social housing tenants. Possilpark on the other hand, comprised dense, and considerably dilapidated, tenement housing, with a predominantly working-class population. By the 1980s they were suffering from the deep recess of deindustrialisation, and come the 1990s, from a heroin epidemic. The *modus operandi* of Jamie Daniels and Eddie Lyons could not have been more different. Indeed, at that point, the Daniels were unlikely to have even been aware of the Lyons (BBC, 1993).

This changed in 2001. However, in reality the seeds had been sown almost a decade earlier. Using his ability to network, and get involved in community happenings, Eddie had managed to form close relationships with both criminals and police. The latter was possibly due to his earlier interactions with police, as well as his coaching position with the local children's amateur football club, Arsenal Boys Club. Indeed, many also suspected Eddie as being a registered police informant. His close relationships with PC John Cameron and PC Peter Glancey, led to many in the community to unofficially calling him 'the special constable' (Findlay, 2012). This relationship with police proved fruitful for Eddie. In the mid-1990s, Eddie gained leadership responsibility for a local community facility, brought about as part of Prime Minister Tony Blair's 'New Labour' initiatives to provide third sector community facilities for local youth in Britain's most deprived areas. Milton in North Glasgow bordered some of these deprived estates: Possilpark to the south; Springburn to the East. Colsten primary school, in Springburn, had closed in 1989, due to deindustrialisation, and a subsequent declining population. It was eventually burned to the ground by arsonists in 1993. However, the school had an annex building just inside the Milton estate, at 342 Ashgill Road. The annex had a range of facilities, including a car park, flood-lit football pitches and internal sporting facilities. The building, owned by Glasgow City Council, was in disuse since 1990. Seizing the opportunity afforded by New Labour policies for providing community facilities to local marginalised populations, PC Cameron spearheaded Police Scotland's efforts to see the annex reopened as a third sector facility. Due to his close relationship with PC Cameron, Eddie Lyons Senior, was nominated, and backed by Strathclyde Police, as a suitable figure to run Chirnsyde Community Club. PC Cameron chaired the board. Just as in Paisley, once again unchecked preferential political treatment sowed the seeds for opportunistic criminal enterprise. These developments were especially ironic and unfortunate given Blair had risen to prominence as Shadow (opposition spokesperson) Home Secretary in July 1993 for claiming the party, if returned to office, would be 'tough on crime, tough on the causes of crime' (BBC, 1993).

CHILD CRIMINAL EXPLOITATION

The Chirnsyde Community Centre was used as a facilitator for child criminal exploitation (CCE). Since the emergence of County Lines drug dealing – involving criminal groups moving illicit drugs across police county borders, typically facilitated by trafficked children – there has been increased awareness around CCE (Densley et al., 2022). Since, 2017, this has significant stimulated academic debate around what CCE actually looks like, given most perceptions are spearheaded by official governmental terminology, regularly adopted in published reports by the National Crime Agency (NCA), and National County Lines Coordination Centre – established as a specialised police response in 2017. Several scholars, social services and institutional bodies (NSPCC, 2023), involved in safeguarding and wraparound services, note children who suffer CCE are often brought into criminal networks by other children. In the case here, Chirnsyde, facilitated the opportunity for Eddie Lyons Senior to enable his own children to bring other youths into his sphere of influence. Given Glasgow's embedded territorialism, Chirnsyde became the local haunt for Milton youth only. Those from Springburn, Possilpark and even those who had residence in the Top-End of the Milton housing estate, were not welcome. Only Bottom-End youth, unofficially speaking, were allowed in. The local youth gang would call themselves 'The Club Boys' (Findlay, 2012a) in reference to their local haunt. As McLean (2019a, 2019b, 2019c) discusses in *Gangs, Drugs and Disorganized Crime*, the premises allowed the Club Boys to look inwards and set clear boundaries as to who was in the gang, and who was not. It also afforded them cover and protection from rival outfits, as well as a figurehead in Eddie Lyons Senior who would support their criminal development under his newly respectable guise. The Club Boys went on to form the backbone of the Lyons crime family, including, in addition to Lyons' own children and wider kinship, Ross Monaghan, Andrew 'Dumbo' Gallacher, Paul McGuinness, Liam Boyle and Charles McMurray, among others (Findlay, 2012b).

The community centre initially operated without any public funds until 1995. Until then, income for maintaining the facility largely came from events held by Eddie Lyons Senior, club members and minor criminality. However, Eddie used his ties to PC Cameron, and local politicians, like Labour Councillor Ellen Hurcombe, to launch successful bids for public money from, the (now defunct), Urban Aid Regeneration fund. Successful bids allowed Eddie Lyons Senior to secure deeper police and political backing, and a steady flow of public money. Eddie Lyons Senior utilised his political and police networks to increase his revenue stream from taxpayer funds. At its height, Eddie Lyons Senior oversaw the allocation of an estimated £2 million per annum: from which he paid himself a handsome wage, employed kinship and purchased a minibus.[2] A notable event that demonstrates the political and police support afforded Eddie Lyons Senior is recalled by Findlay in his account of the attempted murder of Thomas McDonnell (Findlay, 2018), whose sons had suffered a campaign of terror at the hands of the Club Boys. Going to visit Eddie Lyons Senior to plead on his sons' behalf to cease the bullying, Thomas McDonnell entered Chirnsyde on the afternoon of 2 September 2000, only to be confronted by an aggressive Eddie Lyons Senior, who quickly prompted the club boys to assault and stab Mr McDonnell. Mr McDonnell survived. Yet, despite multiple concerns being raised by local residents regarding the incident and Eddie Lyons Senior's credibility, complaints fell on deaf ears. Bridget McConnell (now Lady McConnell of Glenscorrodale), the City Council's then Director of Culture and Leisure Services, was unwilling to launch any internal investigation. Indeed, one of Findlay's interviewees, a local resident of the Milton area, notes over 70 letters of complaint to local MPS and council (wo) men, within a four-year period, all received nil responses in return (Findlay, 2012a).

The assault on Mr McDonnell saw Stephen Lyons charged with attempted murder alongside several others; however, Eddie Lyons Senior persuaded youngster Paul McGuinness to take sole responsibility (Findlay, 2018). He was incarcerated for 8 years. In addition, PC Glancey offered his testimony in support of Eddie Lyons Senior at the court trial. The ability to beat the law only reinforced the youngsters' belief they were untouchable. Spurred on by Eddie Lyons Senior, they used the community centre as a base from which to plan criminal ventures, such as motor theft, robbery and drug supply. Events in 2001, discussed below, only served to see the Lyons crime family grow into a specialised crime syndicate centred upon the illicit supply of drugs.

---

2 While purchased for the centre it was typically parked in Eddie Lyons Senior's residential driveway.

COCAINE THEFT AND PAISLEY PARTNERS

As with the earlier Paisley feud, influencing social and political factors, i.e. political connections, public funding and access firearms, etc., allowed for organised crime to take hold and flourish. The spark that set-in motion the feud to come would arise from issues concerning the efforts to monopolise drug supply. The Daniels had previously taken little notice of the rise of the Lyons. As far as they were concerned they were still retail mid-level dealers at best. Thus, the groups never really crossed paths beyond offering perhaps competitive prices. This would change in August 2001, when Lyons associates, brothers Paul and Mark Mathers, attended a house party at the home of an individual whom the Daniels had paid to store drug consignments in their property (Findlay, 2012a). During the house party, the brothers discovered, and stole, the stored drugs. The drugs were then subsequently sold to the Lyons family directly who divided and distributed it to Club Boys, to sell directly to customers. The Daniels were outraged and launched an investigation into the matter. Interestingly, a Daniels family member wrote a letter demanding payment to the Lyons once again in 2006, following gunmen attack on a Lyons owned business. The letter revealed the amount owed, and read:

> *The boys owe me £25,000 and I want what's owed to me. It's for drugs. They all know what it's about. The money doesn't matter to me as it's got to be paid to the piper. I don't want the police, the boys, not even your wife, knowing about it. If you keep them out of this then all your lives can go back to normal as we are all losing money through this. If you have any tricks for my pickup man then all the deals are off. Remember to keep your mouth shut. No cameras, no surveillance, as the pickup man doesn't know nothing so he's no use to you. Drop off, 4pm Saturday. I'll draw you a map and X will mark the spot. HM Advocate (2022, p. 9)*

The ransom note was delivered via post to the home of David Lyons, and thus is of course dubious as to its credibility, more so given the media coverage of the shootings at the time. Yet, the ransom note claims the amount of money owed to be £25,000, as opposed to the £20,000 which was largely touted in media outlet at the start of feud, prior to the shooting thus may reflect some degree of insider knowledge, lending legitimacy to the letter, and therefore the beginning of the feud (The Herald, 2019). Yet, while the theft of the cocaine undoubtedly lit the fuse for the drug war, wider conditions played a vital part in setting the background. Participant, William, was interviewed as part of the researcher's earlier work. As a mid-level drug dealer, William had extensive ties to the North Glasgow underworld:

> *Paul [Mathers], bumped Daniels gear ... [He] didn't know it was theirs. Might not have made a difference... [he] sold it to [Club Boy member]... Lyons copped the derry for it... In truth, the young Daniels, like Robert boy, had been a bit annoyed but cause the [Club Boys] had been getting a name, and they are kind of the same generation... I didn't know him but, but I heard the chants fae people talking... Robert blamed Lyons, and started going after them, chanting they're dead men.... Lyons didn't do nothing but duck and dive fir a bit... [But] com'on their da[d] was bringing in a fair bit from the [community centre], on top of the drugs they were now selling.... Cause people were going to them to shift product. The Springburn mob, The McGovern's were also shifting brown wi [th] them ... One of their boys started making mates wi[th] a guy Piggy [from Paisley]... Ross [Monaghan] anaw was dating a [female] from [Paisley]... Piggy's mob were older and had been involved in hunners a shootings... [they provided] back up... getting shooters, bodies, that... Daniels didn't like that... it became you hit us, we hit you back.*

Williams's statement is resounded in multiple sources, including media reports (McKay, 2017), documentaries (Documentary City, 2022) and autobiographical accounts (Findlay, 2012a). In addition to the theft of cocaine, William sheds light on the situation more broadly. William notes, the war was not simply the result of theft, but rather wider social and environmental factors had set the background over time. The theft simply provided the spark to set it off. The fact the Lyons had a steady stream of income from taping into taxpayers money meant they, like FCB earlier, had a premises to collect and store drugs, a visible contact point for sellers and buyers, and legitimate steady income to purchase drugs in bulk, as opposed to on debt or 'tick' (McLean, 2019a, 2019b, 2019c). The revenue from the taxpayer gave the Lyons something worth fighting for, as opposed to fold to Daniel pressure. Yet consistently being targeted by the Daniels meant they would be forced to seek alliances: forging social and business relationships with the McGovern's and more so their paisley counterparts, who brought invaluable experience and resources to fight back. During the beginnings of the feud, several key players involved in the Paisley drug war would be released from prison, notably Robert Pickett and William Burns several years later.

Indeed, their first response to consistent Daniels attacks came via the Paisley partnership. After Robert Daniel initially responded to the theft by issuing verbal and written threats, he along with peers, would carry out a series of low-level incidents including vandalism of the community centre and bus, along with minor assaults on Lyons associates. These attacks were largely ad hoc. Robert Daniel's friend Kevin Carroll, who was also the long-term partner of his sister Kelly Green, was largely the main protagonist and would specifically hunt Lyons members down, often touring Milton in a vehicle seeking out would be victims. A written prison letter from William at the time supports this:

> He hates all [Lyons and associates] ... I seen he had [Lyons associate] stab[ed]... in the [stomach]. Don't know what the fuck he really has tae dae wi it all... [and] tried to run over [Stephen Lyons friend]... [Carrol's] fucking loopy.

William's written prison correspondence to his sibling at the time supports wider claims that he was targeting all Lyons associates in a campaign of hatred. As attacks gradually intensified, in September 2001, Kevin Carroll attempted to gun down Stephen Lyons outside Mallon's, a pub in the north side of the city. He was not hit so survived the attack; the Lyons were forced to respond.

TARGETED ATTACKS

Following the attempted assassination of Stephen Lyons, the Lyons turned to their new partners in Paisley for support and guidance (Findlay, 2012a). Pickett put the Lyons in contact with a gun for hire in Stephen Burgess. On 12 January 2003 the Lyons gunned Carroll down outside his family home in Drumchapel (Silvester, 2022). Upon leaving his mother's house, Carroll, then walking his dog, towards his friend Barry Kelly's, car, was pounced upon by Stephen Burgess. Armed with a shotgun, Burgess chased Carroll and shot him twice in the leg. Carroll fell and at Burgess's subsequent trial testified: 'I was lying on the ground and the gunman was standing over me. He ran away when my mum came running out of her house' (Findlay, 2012a). Due to lack of evidence and cooperation, the case was thrown out. Several days later, the Daniels retaliated and targeted Johnny Lyons at his home in Milton (Findlay, 2010). Carroll along with a colleague approached Johnny's home in Stornoway Street, and opened fire after knocking on the front door. Johnny spoke publicly of the incident, but provided little information other than beyond acknowledging his extensive criminal ties.

Targeting Carroll became the Lyons strategy for shifting the power balance, more so after fellow antagonist Robert Daniel was incarcerated for the supply of heroin: a crime he would repeat and subsequently be jailed for again in 2022 (Walker, 2022). Carroll however continued to target Lyons members, and opened fire on Lyons associate John Madden on 10 January 2004, with an AK-47 (Findlay, 2010). While visiting brothers Brian and Andrew Ferguson, Madden arrived at their home in his work van. Upon arrival, Carroll approached the van holding the automatic firearm. Set at semi-automatic setting, Carroll fired several shots into the vehicle, shattering the front windscreen and striking Madden on the shoulder. The firearm was never recovered, yet a haul of AK-47 cartridges were later found at the home of a Carroll associate during a police raid (Findlay, 2012a). On 18 April 2006, Carroll and Raymond Anderson, used a 'doubler' vehicle and drove to the home of Eddie Lyons Senior in Cumbernauld. Lyons had relocated there after growing violence in Milton. Parking outside the home, Carroll remained in the vehicle, while Anderson, in a ski mask, exited the vehicle and knocked on the home door. Upon answering, Eddie Lyons Junior, then 28, quickly realised the gravity of the situation, and attempted to slam the door shut. By then Anderson had fired the shotgun. Luckily for Eddie Lyons Junior, the front door absorbed the brunt of the force, and he survived. Anderson and Carroll quickly made off. The doubler would be found touched on Auchinarin Road (McAlpine, 2006). Again, due to lack of witness cooperation, the police were unable to mount any case.

Carroll followed this attack up in early November 2006. Again with Anderson, the pair drove to an ambush location to shoot Eddie Lyons Junior, after a tip off by a drug dealer who owed Eddie money (Findlay, 2012a). On route to collect the money, Eddie Lyons Junior and Andrew Gallacher dove into a small cul-de-sac, at Myers court in Bellshill, North Lanarkshire. Upon exiting their vehicle, Carroll, crouched and stepping out from behind a row of wheeled bins, fired a shotgun. Eddie Lyons Junior sped off unharmed in his BMW X5. Andrew Gallacher however was shot by Carroll but survived due to wearing a bullet proof vest. A week later, the Lyons hit back. Meeting associate Craig Gallagher, at a quiet street in Bishopbriggs, Carroll and associate Ross Sherlock pulled up in Sherlock's BMW X5, to chat. Yet gaining information of the meeting, the Lyons piled into two doubler vehicles, making haste to the location around 10 p.m. As the vehicles turned into the street the passengers exited and off-loaded a barrage of shots in Carroll's direction. Both Carroll and Sherlock, still seated in Sherlock's vehicle, were struck by bullets in their torsos and legs. Amazingly, an unmarked police vehicle had been following Carroll and the policemen inside saw the event unfold.

However, unarmed and startled, they were unable to respond. Carroll claimed police corruption and, outraged, retaliated only a few days later with the Applerow massacre incident, which opened this book, in early December 2006.

The Applerow incident brought widespread public attention to the Daniels-Lyon feud, and as such with mounting police and political pressure, Eddie Lyons Senior's legitimate allies could no longer ignore requests to have him removed from the community centre. On 7th December 2006, one day after Applerow, police and council vehicles arrived at the Chirnsyde community centre. Entering the building, Eddie Lyons Senior, his family members and other associated figures, were informed to take their personal belongings and get out. Media outlets would be filled in the coming days with the true extent of political corruption and violence. *Sunday Times* journalist Joan McAlpine (a future SNP MSP) wrote the headline 'This is a nasty stink you cannot just ignore, Jack' in reference to the level of political incompetence and corruption which had benefited Eddie Lyons Senior. The column stated:

> *[Labour First Minister of Scotland] Jack McConnell is publicly committed to fighting crime… yet his wife's department, and his party organisation in Glasgow, has given a man with high-profile criminal associates £1.4m in public funds… Lyons family involved in in a long-running feud with another group of villains, the Daniels, and at least 11 people have been shot since 2003 as a result of this vendetta.…. It sounds like something you might expect to find in the slums of Rio, but the astonishing aspect of this debacle is the authorities' complacency. I first came across the story in 2003, when I heard that local parents were complaining that the council was forcing them to send their children to after school fitness classes at Chirnsyde. McConnell was… inundated with letters. Yet nothing was done until 2005, when she produced a report claiming there was no evidence of criminal activity or misuse of funds. Sunday Times (2006)*

Political corruption undoubtedly helped fuel the feud. Even when Lyons supporter Bridget McConnell – Jack's wife – suggested perhaps Eddie Lyons Senior be removed, four months prior to his eviction, Labour councillor Steven Purcell, vetoed the associated motion (Findlay, 2012a). It later emerged Purcell, who as Leader of the council from 2005–2010 oversaw the city's £2 billion per annum budget, was indebted to the Lyons. In 2010 Purcell resigned as a Councillor in 2010 citing stress and exhaustion. Due to firearms charges, Carroll's vendetta against the Lyons would be put on hold for several years, due to his short-term incarceration.

Asda Assassination

While the Daniels crime family deployed similar tactics to those used by warring factions in Paisley a decade earlier, whereby anyone and everyone affiliated with rival groups were potential targets, the Lyons were more astute in their efforts. Drawing upon their Paisley alliances, the young Lyons members were able to tap into the lived and learned experience of hardened criminals, like Pickett. Rather than attack indiscriminately, the Lyons targeted individuals operating key roles in linchpin areas essential to the Daniel powerbase. Given Jamie Daniel was near impossible to pin down in order to set an ambush, and Robert Daniel was imprisoned, they would target Daniels enforcer Kevin Carroll following his release. This plan of action was first implemented via Burgess. The second attempt occurred following the shooting of Carroll and Sherlock while seated in Sherlock's vehicle. The third attempt, however, succeeded.

In the early afternoon of 13 January 2010, Asda's Robroyston carpark, in broad day light, saw busy shoppers went about their daily business, involuntary witnesses to a shift in Scotland's criminal underworld. Russell Findlay recounts Court testimony and details the following interaction in significant depth (Findlay, 2012a). Following a meeting with Carrol, Steven Glen of Springburn, witnessed the results of the crucial information he had passed on the night before to associates. The day before the shooting, Glen had received a phone call from a withheld number. Upon answering, the voice was recognisable. Glen, filled with a sense of dread, acceded to Carrol's demands for a face-to-face meeting the next day, to discuss the sale of drugs. Glen had worked somewhat independently selling cocaine, and raked in a handsome earning of around £250,000 annually. Now Carrol sought to muscle in on Glen's business. Frightened and fearful he might fall prey to Carrols 'alien abduction squad', who kidnapped and tortured underworld figures due to their lack of recourse to law, in an attempt to rob victims of their illegal goods, Glen turned to associates for help. They included Allan 'Babesy' Johnston: a former police office turned gangster. Carrol's bullying behaviour meant he was a feared, yet hated figure in the criminal underworld.

During the briefest of meetings around 1:20 p.m. outside the main entrance of Asda, Carrol informed Glen he now 'worked' for him (BBC News, 2012). Glen would receive £10,000 a month in return. The terms were non-negotiable and refusal would mean death. Leaving the meeting, Carrol and his associates, John Bonner and Stephen McLaggan, returned to their parked vehicle, a black three door Audi. Upon reaching the car, Bonner entered the driver's front door, while McLaggan opened the passenger's front door: lifting the seat forward for Carrol to enter the backseats: to retain a low profile. As the passenger seat clicked back into place, effectively locking Carrol in, and before McLaggan could enter the vehicle, a VW Golf sped up and slammed on the breaks in front of the parked Audi. The Audi was boxed in with parked cars on either side of the parking bay. Two masked individuals exited the now stationary VW Golf. One armed with a silver-coloured Strum Ruger SP101 revolver, the other with a Croatian manufactured HS Produkt HS 95. The men flanked the left and right of the Audi. Fearing for their lives, Carrolls associates had fled the scene on foot. Carroll was locked in the backseat. Th men proceeded to fire a barrage of bullets through either side window. Carrol's cheekbone and skull were shattered in the attack, and several vital organs punctured. Within 45 seconds, the attack was over, leaving the 29-year-old Kevin Carroll strewn across the backseat of the Audi, riddled with bullet holes. His assailants, suspected to be Ross Monaghan, then 30, and William Patterson, then 35, struck Carrol with a total 13 bullets, before fleeing the scene in the VW Golf.

The following month Jamie Daniel would be given a short jail sentence for a road rage attack. As it was unlike Jamie to act so carelessly, it is presumed the pressure of the feud got to him. He eventually died of cancer in 2016. Yet the Lyons-Daniels feud had not ended; it simply changed direction.

CHAPTER SUMMARY

This chapter traced the political socio-economical and cultural factors which contributed to the explosion of drug-related organised crime in Paisley and South Glasgow repeated, but this time in a different place context. The same factors which arose in Paisley, manifested again, but within a different context and thus saw history repeat itself. The Lyons v Daniels drug war in Glasgow was very much a repeat of history as the Scottish government, local councils and Police Scotland failed to learn from prior lessons. While the drug war in Glasgow came to define the criminal landscape of Scotland in many ways, it was ultimately very much avoidable.

7

CONCLUSION AND POLICY LESSONS

CHAPTER INTRODUCTION

Many anticipated the death of Gerbil and Jamie Daniels, along with the incarceration of several key members of their organisation, to effectively result in the end of Scotland's drug wars. It was recognised that smaller feuds would continue to some extent, albeit to a much lesser degree. However, the opposite occurred, whereby prior tension applied to the criminal groups, from each other, alternative fractions and from law enforcement, resulting in increased group sophistication, organisation and proliferation. Thus, both quasi-Daniels and quasi-Lyons style criminal groups emerged in the early 2010s and continued in an ongoing drug war. Other criminals would stepped in and tapped into international criminal networks to increase profitability, product availability and access to military grade firearms. This chapter explores how these events unfolded.

AFTERMATH

The 1990s marked the advent of the Paisley drug war. This arose through political negligence and corruption, which allowed criminals to access legitimate revenue streams, local premises and council contracts. Organised criminal groups used these resources in their efforts to monopolise illegal drug market-based enterprises over local competitors. The pattern was repeated in the 2000s, in Glasgow, with the Daniels and Lyons drug war – again, brought about through political corruption and financial mismanagement. These factors gave the Lyons a reason and foothold to challenge, and fight, their competitors, in efforts to monopolise the local drug trade. The decade from

2010 until 2020, saw a significant change in how drug-based organised crime would unfold and extrapolate across Scotland. Despite the eventual death of Jamie Daniel in 2016, and the assignation of Carroll earlier in 2011, alongside the long-term incarceration of several key members of the Daniels crime family, no end to the drug wars have materialised. Rather, since then quasi-Daniels and Lyons style criminal groups have emerged to dominate Scotland's criminal landscape. They have evolved into two of the largest and most sophisticated criminal outfits in Britain at this writing. Several factors would play important roles in creating these successor criminal groups.

By the end of 2011, the Lyons certainly held the upper hand and given that the Club Boys were bounded by the extension of territoriality, and not kinship alone. This meant they could replace key members much quicker than the Daniels. In addition, it also meant that they were able to bring others into the fold from further afield and regularly done so, forging criminal alliances across the central belt and into Edinburgh and the East Coast. In response the Daniels did likewise, albeit a tad slower than their competitors. Although the Daniels forged fewer alliances, these were likely more potent ones, with key personnel in the criminal underworld, including Mark Richardson in Edinburgh (The Herald, 2017) and successful business entrepreneur Stevie Malcolm (Alexander, 2014).

In 2016, with the passing of Jamie Daniel, a void emerged in the underworld (McGivern, 2016). This void was not filled by the Lyons, however, as anticipated, but by the cross-country partnership the Daniels had established with other actors. Throughout the war between either side, alliances had been forged. Other criminal groups and affiliations were forced to support one side or the other, such was the groups' mutual hatred. Much of those alliances, loyal to the Daniels remained active after the passing of Jamie Daniels. However, rather than being forged around Jamie Daniel, these partnerships would come to work in greater efficiently with one another. During Jamie Daniels reign, the importation of drugs had come from several sources, out with his own traffickers. Heroin came from his contacts in the Asian community. Cannabis from his contacts forged earlier with Mr P in Paisley and cocaine from the Gillespie brothers. It is the Gillespie brothers this chapter focuses on, especially how they managed to step into the void left behind by Jamie Daniels in organising, to even greater efficiency, the partnerships left behind. These were recognised as 'Scotland's most Sophisticated Criminal Gang' (BBC, 2018b).

Originally hailing from the town of Rutherglen, South Lanarkshire, James and Barry Gillespie, simply known as 'The Brothers' in the criminal underworld, had gained considerable reputations throughout their early adult years as violent criminals and capable drug dealers (BBC, 2023b). During these early years, the pair forged strong alliances with several criminal outfits in the neighbouring towns throughout Lanarkshire, and in particular the notorious Glasgow estate of Castlemilk (BBC, 2022). In 2004 the pair were suspected of killing martial arts instructor Mark Toner, from Pollokshaws (BBC, 2015). Toner had become indebted to The Brothers over a drug dispute. In a series of incidents prior to his murder, Toner had several physical altercations with the pair. In one incident Toner had managed to disarm one of the two brothers, stabbing him in the neck with his own knife. The Gillespies swore revenge for this attack. No one has ever been convicted of Toner's killing, although it is widely suspected that the Gillespies were responsible and fled the country shortly after (Silvester, 2021). Now relocated overseas, with homes in Spain and Portugal, the pair pursued their criminal entrepreneur ambition of becoming major drug traffickers. The Brothers were able to, initially, tap into criminal networks with other overseas Brits and economic migrants who had fled to Costa Del Sol to avoid justice over the years, later setting up new links with criminal groups based in South America (BBC, 2023a). These links allowed the Gillespie brothers to become large-scale importers, primarily of cocaine, for other criminal groups in Glasgow, including Jamie Daniels', as well as continuing to supply their own group based in Castlemilk. The links to South American criminal gangs in Rio De Janeiro further enabled The Brothers to access military grade firearms. Some of these, including frag grenades and Skorpion machine guns, would be sent to Scotland. The Brothers had been on the police radar for a number of years even before their demise in 2022 (BBC, 2017).

In 2009, French police confiscated 684 kg of pure cocaine with a street value of over £30,000,000 from a haulage truck bound for Scotland (Alexander, 2009). The truck was owned by Uddingston-based logistics business owner, and Gillespie associate, Charles McAughey. McAughey denied any knowledge that his trucks were being used by drivers to traffic drugs. Eventually the driver and passenger of the vehicle were incarcerated for their role in trafficking, yet underworld and police sources suspected the Brothers to be responsible for these large-scale arrangements and shipments of illegal drugs (Alexander, 2009). Yet, the true extent of their influence over the country's illicit drugs trade was not revealed before the abduction and torture of drug dealer Robert Allan, and the apprehension of cocaine drug dealer, and Edinburgh underworld kingpin, Mark Richardson in 2018 (in the Baillieston area of Glasgow) (BBC, 2018c). These two crucial events revealed the Brothers to have pulled together former Daniel associates and partners and headed the criminal organisation from their base overseas. They used their own criminal organisation in Castlemilk, along with their extensive network throughout Lanarkshire, to ensure that transactions of cash, product and weaponry flowed smoothly.

APPREHENDING SCOTLAND'S MOST SOPHISTICATED GANG

In March 2015, low level drug dealer Robert Allan, heard his door, in Barnsley, South Yorkshire, being knocked in the late hours of the night. Upon answering the door, he recognised the visitor as David Sell. Mr Sell was accompanied by two other men, both unknown to Robert. Entering the house, in an orderly but forceful manner, Mr Sell strolled directly into the living room and sat on the centrepiece couch before producing a handgun. Robert was informed by Mr Sell that he would be escorted to a preassigned location to be questioned about an outstanding drug debt of approximately £45,000, owed to an associate of Mr Sell. In addition, he would be punished for the inconvenience caused to Mr Sell and those he was acting on the behalf of James and Barry Gillespie. As Robert pleaded for more time to acquire the funds to pay the debt, Mr Sell stated 'it's not about the money. it's the fucking principle' (McCabe, 2017). There was also perhaps apprehension on Mr Sell's part to allocate more time given that Mr Allan had discreetly relocated to his new address, from Scotland, to avoid payment and detection, yet was traced through criminal networks. After a brief scuffle, Mr Allan was subsequently bound in chains and driven to a desolate industrial estate Fauldhouse, Midlothian. He would be held, bound, blindfolded and tortured.

During the ordeal, Mr Sell would guard Mr Allan, while the other two individuals punched and kicked him mercilessly. In addition, Mr Allan would be whipped with a thick metal chain repeatedly over the head and body. One of his legs was broken, deliberately, after being assaulted with a 14-pound sledgehammer. A fourth individual who appeared at the site would also produce a gun and carry out mock executions and threats on Mr Allan's life. A fifth individual, who likewise later appeared on the scene, ordered that the victim be stripped for humiliating purposes and sprayed with a bleach in order to cause further pain on his already sustained injuries. The latter was suspected as being one of the Gillespie brothers. A hooded Mr Allan was then transported and dumped on a rural spot near East Kilbride, Scotland. Before being dumped though he would be shot three times. Twice in one knee and once in the other.

Conclusion and Policy Lessons 93

Mr Allan recovered from his ordeal and give testimony at Glasgow's High Court in 2018. Mr Allan was able to give evidence after police managed to link his DNA to a Beretta used to pistol-whip him during his ordeal. The Baretta had been recovered following an ongoing police operation, Escalade, which has been running since 2014. As part of the operation, police had been monitoring properties, vehicles and the movements of those linked to the Daniels and now the Gillespies. Through an act of good fortune, a breakthrough moment came on 20 January 2017. Police Chief Superintendent Gerry McLean recalled the moment for a BBC report on events:

> *Two officers were watching a silver Yaris in Church Street, Baillieston, on the eastern outskirts of Glasgow, when they spotted Mark Richardson… Intelligence had linked the Edinburgh-based gangster with the group but this was a chance encounter that changed everything. The Yaris had been part of the surveillance operation but Richardson's arrest was the moment it switched from a covert to an overt operation. The officers gave chase and he was eventually rugby-tackled to the ground. Richardson had the Yaris keys on him. We noticed a fob which did not appear to activate any alarm on the Toyota. The detectives discovered there was a Bluetooth device in the rear cluster light of the car and the fob activated it. When you activated the Bluetooth receiver there was a metal plate in the boot of the Yaris which came up on a hydraulic ram. Within that they found a neoprene holster containing a 9mm Glock 17 handgun.* BBC (2018b)

The arrest set in motion a chain of events which unravelled a vast criminal network. Further keys were linked to an industrial units across Glasgow, where £250,000 worth of modified vehicles were found to contain Glock pistols, a Heckler and Koch sub-machine gun, M75 hand grenade among other firearms, drugs and concealed cash (BBC, 2018b). The investigation resulted in the eventual arrest and incarceration of 13 gang members in total, including known gunrunner Martyn Fitzsimmons of Clydebank near Glasgow, wholesale drug dealer Barry O'Neil from Glasgow and Edinburgh cocaine kingpin Mark Richardson.[1] It identified links to Anthony Beard who worked with the gang in providing false passports allowing gang members to flee overseas – several were arrested in Brazil and the Netherlands (BBC, 2023a). The Gillespie brothers

---
[1] Indeed, a number of the individuals were known criminals with lengthy convictions and criminal charges for other offenses, prior to their involvement with this particular organised criminal group.

however remain at large. The pair though are thought to have been abducted and killed in Brazil after initially seeking refuge among their South American criminal associates, while fleeing from UK and European law enforcement agencies. It is believed that the Brazil criminal organisation raised the fees to maintain their protection. Following failure to pay, the pair were subsequently abducted and killed. Law enforcement has been successful however in apprehending other main players involved in the Gillespie chain of command. Indeed, James White, originally from Glasgow, operated as a linchpin between The Brothers and their UK associates but was arrested in Fortaleza, Brazil, in June 2020. Once sent back to Scotland on drug trafficking and firearm charges, at the High Court in Stirling, Lord Colbeck incarcerated White for almost 10 years. Alongside other members of his family, Jordon Owens, from Castlemilk, had been an enforcer for the organisation, and was jailed in 2022 for shooting Jamie Lee. Owens used his contacts to flee to Portugal but was picked up in 2019 in Lisbon and sent back to the United Kingdom for sentencing – being given a 23-year sentence (McCabe, 2022). Along with several other key arrests, the Gillespie's operation effectively came to an end. At their height though, Scotland's most sophisticated gang were estimated to have had a financial intake of approximately £2,000,000 per month from their drug-related activities (BBC, 2018b). Despite being labelled Scotland's most sophisticated criminal gang, the Lyons remained active and sought to eliminate this quasi-Daniel style group. While Stephen Lyons relocated to Dubai and married into the Irish Kinahan crime family, other key Lyons members including Brian Ferguson, Andrew Gallacher, Robert Pickett, Andrew Sinclair, John Hardie and Peter Bain were incarcerated in 2021, for approximately a century between them, for systematically targeting Daniels members and associates and permanently disfiguring (often with machete attacks) or shooting them (Mulholland, 2021).

Since 2018, Scotland has consistently been at the forefront of Europe's drug deaths tabulations (Scottish Government, 2023). Indeed, bar one exception, Glasgow has always led the figures.[2] The National Record of Scotland report, *Drug-related deaths in Scotland in 2022*, found most deaths to be linked to an embedded drug culture of poly drug use (National Records of Scotland, 2023). Heroin deaths have decline in recent years but have been replaced by deaths linked to home manufactured Valium, known as 'street' or 'fake' Valium, and also cocaine. Recent arrests have revealed a number of criminals used or owned small business and factory premises to press their own pills using pill press machinery (McGivern, 2018). Furthermore, while alive the Gillespie brothers were at the forefront of advertising a criminal network, EncroChat

---

[2] Even then it was a close second to the city of Dundee.

(NCA, 2020). EncroChat was a Europe-based communications network and service provider that offered modified smartphones allowing encrypted communication among subscribers (Sky News, 2020). It was used primarily by organised crime members to plan criminal activities. Police infiltrated the network between at least March and June 2020, during a Europe-wide investigation. An unidentified source associated with EncroChat announced on the night of 12–13 June 2020 that the company would cease operations because of the police operation. At the time of its closure it had roughly 60,000 members. The chat enabled any criminal with access to these dedicated mobile phones, to contact other criminals across the country and even abroad, to purchase and sell drugs at various quantity levels. The chat was also used by criminals to put out contracts for rival criminals to be assaulted or killed, as in the case of Edinburgh-based Sean Orman who accepted a £10,000 contract from Edinburgh-based Lyons affiliate George 'Dode' Baigrie to assassinate Bradley Welsh, an associate of Mark Richardson (BBC, 2021).

CONCLUDING DISCUSSION

Having read this far, readers are broadly current with the organised criminal landscape in Scotland as of 2024, and how such developments have long been in process. They can be traced to the 1980s, when criminal gangs began to centralise and reorganise themselves around drug-based criminality. This book will now move to its conclusion, which revisits the purpose of the book and in doing so delineates further areas of research that should be taken up or at least considered by other researchers. This includes consideration of this study's limitations. No book is definitive, but this one considered the development of drug-based organised crime down a particular narrative and pathway. This is a narrative which of course will, and should, be contested. Only in doing so, will research further refine itself through the tension and rebuttal that is applied. No single study has ever concluded everything within its boundaries of discussion; further studies, whether complementary or challenging, are the lifeblood of academic research.

The book began, after the prologue of the Applerow murders (an especially violent public manifestation of drug-related organised crime), by overviewing the development of organised crime in Scotland and tracing the shift from predatory crimes (against people) to market-based crime in illegal drugs. This book drew on ethnographic fieldwork undertaken by the first author as part of his doctoral studies, as well as collaborative research generated by the first author in collaboration with Robinson, Densely and the second author Chris Holligan. The fieldwork was primarily conducted with small group interviewees in and around Glasgow and neighbouring Renfrewshire, but included some interviews in Ayrshire, Edinburgh, the Highlands and the Western Isles. The fieldwork was informed by the oral history framework set out by Lynn Abrams (2010), focusing more on the *meanings* derived by interviewees from their lived experience than on facts and events, albeit the latter were corroborated and contextualised with reference to print sources where relevant. Publicly available official and newspaper sources were complemented by archival research including letters and diaries of participants in the illegal drugs trade in West Scotland. Among the interviewees were notable figures in Paisley's 1990s criminal underworld. Published autobiographies of key underworld figures were also consulted.

The book moved on, in chapter two, to review key literature in the intersecting areas of organised crime and drug markets. This included the changing terminology associated with these social phenomena. Organised crime was considered at the international level before the focus narrowed to Europe, the United Kingdom and Scotland. Efforts to quantify the size and scope of the illegal drugs trade were discussed. This set the scene for chapter three, where the illegal drug trade in Glasgow and west Scotland was examined in considerable detail. The origins and development of Glasgow, and the nearby town of Paisley, were traced in a manner highlighting their reliance on industry and, resultingly, their populations' vulnerability to the shocks associated with deindustrialisation in the late 20th century. The chapter examined the shift from criminal (knife) gang activity to drug-related organised crime in the city and its environs in the second half of the 20th century, with a particular focus on the links between unemployment and criminal activity, as well as territoriality and masculinity. Territoriality and conceptions of masculinity were consistent between the eras of knife gangs and the illegal drug trade. Chapter three also considered the overlapping spheres of 'glocal' markets both legal and illegal, and the potential for local and national government to lend legitimacy to the latter, for example through the regulation of private hire taxis and security firms. The blurring of legitimate and illegitimate market activity proved fertile ground for the development of drug-related organised crime analysed in the second half of the book, especially after the 1980s heroin boom.

Chapter 4 moved on to consider the development of the drug trade in Paisley, which represented a bridgehead for drug-based organised crime in Glasgow and Scotland more widely. It began by examining the criminal career of 'Mr P' (K). K adroitly navigated the legal and illegal connections between Paisley and Glasgow, through networking and facilitating accommodations between leaders of rival criminal 'families' including Brockwell and Ferris. He forged new illegal drug supply routes from Paisley into Glasgow, and from Glasgow to other parts of Scotland. The chapter proceeded to accounts of the criminal careers of James Daniels and Frank McPhie, moving on to consider the rise and conflict between the Daniels and Lyons families. The chapter emphasised that these careers did not occur in a socio-economic and political vacuum, but were, rather, intricately connected to rising unemployment and residualisation of housing stock in Paisley's Ferguslie Park scheme. Housing stock residualisation was a direct consequence of the UK Thatcher government's policy, formalised in the Housing Act (1980) of selling off public housing to private owners, resulted in 'ghettoization' of areas like Ferguslie Park. This, coupled with increased unemployment, precipitated a perfect storm, whereby those affected turned to drugs for mental escape from their predicament, or to criminal employment for their livelihood (the two options were by no means mutually exclusive). Ferguslie Park Community Business (FCB) security and the scandal surrounding it all but epitomised the connections between neoliberal 'enterprise' promotion by the UK state, local government corruption and drug-based organised crime in a distinctively Paisley pattern. Chapter five then examined the 1990s drug wars between criminal gangs in Paisley and Glasgow. It explores how the Gillespie gang, in their newly legitimised form of FCB security, was able to consolidate their dominance over the Ferguslie Park estate and its illegal drugs market. FCB used drug debts (real or claimed) and their company payroll to launder the proceeds of their illegal drugs sales. They also used buildings in their charge as de facto firearms arsenals.

Chapter 6 showed how the emergent trafficking class which established supply in Paisley and resulted in local criminal groups reorganise around drug supply, was subsequently replicated in the north of Glasgow by the early 2000s, with the new drugs war between the Lyons and Daniels crime families. Here again, the interacting roles of UK Government, as well as devolved Scottish Executive (now Scottish Government) policies and corrupt (or at best misguided and naïve) local government implementation (by Glasgow City Council), played its role in facilitating drug-related organised crime's development and façade of legitimacy. In the case of Eddie Lyons' civically endorsed and funded youth work at Chirnsyde the result was child criminal exploitation. The chapter moved on to consider the violent denouement of the Daniels-Lyons drug war. Throughout the chapter, missed opportunities to reduce the criminogenic potential of the long half-life of deindustrialisation into the New Labour era are emphasised. In that spirit, the discussion moves now, after considering the book's research strengths and limitations, to positive policy lessons that might be drawn from this book's research basis.

Research Strengths and Limitations

This book's purpose has been to draw attention to the manner in which criminals in Scotland since the 1980s, who were once deemed to be professionals, have steadily become entrenched within, and centralised around, highly organised drug-based criminality. In doing so, they have made marked shift from broadly predatory crimes to market-based crimes. In doing so, the authors deemed it vitally important to highlight those factors and mistakes that have continually contributed to the refinement of these criminal gangs. It is true that social and economic factors beyond the control of any particular political party, such as deindustrialisation, poor housing and amenities and lack of job security and income more generally in the country, have contributed to increased criminality. Many of the factors which have had significant input in propelling these criminal gangs to the status they operate today, with millions of pounds and military grade weaponry at their disposal, have simply been facilitated by political ineptitude at best, corruption and complicity at worst.

For example, earlier chapters showed that in the original criminal feuds in the town of Paisley during the 1980s and 1990s were largely due to the local government corruption. Mismanagement of public funds, intended to help the economically hardest hit communities, such as Ferguslie Park, were in fact knowingly deflected into the pockets of local gangsters. The steady flow of cash, resources and legitimisation of their criminal conduct, only resulted in gangs like those headed by Stuart Gillespie and Stuart Boyd to not only create footholds for monopolising drug trade. They were seen by the wider public to have the backing, to some degree, of local politicians and those holding key positions within local authorities at the time. Effectively, this legitimation of one criminal group over others helps establish a sense of superiority – in many respects they become the untouchables. A decade later, history repeated itself in north Glasgow. In earlier years, other upcoming criminal groups in north Glasgow may have taken a backseat after being pitted against the Daniels crime group, who had a fearsome reputation in the underworld. But they lacked, and did not seek, any political or police legitimisation. Once again the mismanagement and misallocation of public funds into the pockets of, this time the Lyons crime family, simply resulted in the young Club Boys having

Conclusion and Policy Lessons

something worth fighting for. The allocation of public funds, a premises, a mini-van and storage units for drugs, effectively gave the Lyons a patch of territory, a foothold if you will, within the district of Milton. In addition, being given political and local council backing, alongside police corruption, allowed the Lyons to gain a sense of legitimacy. In turn they were able to fight back, challenge and even overtake other criminal groups in the area. The effects of politically inept, fraudulent allocation of public funds, and wider corruption, are evident for all to see. The criminals involved in these events are of course to culpable for the death of many and destruction of local community values. Yet the very organisations tasked with keeping criminals at bay were in fact active contributors to their actions and success – setting the foundations and parameters for almost inevitable drug wars.

While a key objective of this book was to highlight these flaws in the vain hope that the same mistakes are not made over and over, the research of course is not without its limitations. An evident limitation is the focus on a west of Scotland narrative. This narrative was driven by wider factors such as the disproportionate amount of organised crime and drugs harms that occurred within the region, as evidenced by official government and police reports and documentation. A decade's worth of the first author's research from the field, suggested events such as those that occurred in 1980s Paisley played a significant role in the origins of criminal gang reorganisation around drug-based organised crime in Scotland. Still, other events may have occurred in various regions of the country which may have had significant influence on future gang reorganisation in Scotland, but simply did not feature within the limited knowledge of the researchers and available official documentation. In addition, key hubs for drug importation into Britain, such as Liverpool, underwent similar experiences to those that occurred in the west of Scotland, during the same period of time, and lie outside this short volume's scope.

Therefore, the interaction, overlap and intertwined nature of these events are not fully covered herein, although at times alluded to. It is well known, for example that Stuart Boyd, as discussed within the context of this book, sourced drugs from a select few high-end criminal gangs operating in Liverpool and Manchester on several occasions. Yet the secrecy around these interactions, the lack of extant archival and other sources of evidence, makes it near impossible to shed light as to how these arrangements directly impacted on developments in Scotland, beyond simple statements that collections of product were made in exchange for money. Such exchanges may have incurred other features not really explored such as alternative forms of currency, information or favours, including gangland assassinations (See Rahman et al., 2022). Therefore, the book is by no means ignorant of the fact that wider occurrences throughout the length and breadth of the United Kingdom would have impacted on developments in and around the Glasgow conurbation, but rather the scope of the book, research and narrative taken does not delve into such developments in any great depth. Rather limiting the discussion to Scotland has been applied intentionally, simply to present a story specific to the country, which others can follow and develop comparable analysis to, should they wish.

Another limitation of the research is of course the selection of the data itself. While objectivity is desired, in reality all research is subjective to some extent in its selection and methods. This is even truer when applied to the use of qualitative data, as utilised here. While the data is derived from several studies to have occurred over the last 10 years or more, the range of, and access to, particular participants may inevitably paint a specific type of picture detailing selected types of criminality and events. The researchers here primarily had access to criminals, former offenders and practitioners who operate within the field of drug harms and distribution; therefore, the data itself tends to present a picture on this very topic. Yet the nexus with other types of criminality may be overlooked as a result. For example, in discussing the Winters crime family, who were heavily involved in the drugs trade in the Renfrewshire area during the 1980s and 1990s, other aspects of criminality are overlooked, neglected or missed, such as the sexual offences of gang member James Winters. These events cannot always be assumed as completely distinct of one another in all cases. Other examples are evident throughout the book. Other criminals, such as those involved in human trafficking and the sex trade were not accessible to the researchers, or when they were, discussions on such issues were not pursued but rather attention was given to drug harms. Therefore, it is by no means a given that such types of crimes are not prevalent, or impact on other areas of criminality, either. The interviews undertaken and official sources sought as part of the research, created a picture that criminal gangs in Scotland have over the last few decades become centred on drug-based crimes, but other aspects of crime, other types of market-based criminality and the nexus between these operations require further investigation.

Other constraints on the research are perhaps more obvious. Constraints relating to both time and cost, alongside scope and boundary, very much impacted on the research findings presented here. This book was written in conjunction with studies undertaken by the first author, who enroled on a yearlong Masters in Research (MRes) in the discipline of History at Strathclyde University in 2022. As such, the scale of the project was significantly smaller than that of the researcher's prior doctoral dissertation in 2019. Monographs tend to be written following completion of anywhere between a three- to five-year project, typically speaking, as part doctoral studies. Therefore, the amount of knowledge input into the book, derived from the MRes, cannot be compared directly with, for example the amount of knowledge put in McLean, 2019a, 2019b, 2019c monograph *Gangs, Drugs and Disorganised Crime*. While prior interviews from earlier studies, including the first researchers doctoral research, were brought into this book, to support wider claims, statements and overarching narratives, it must be recognised that earlier studies did not solely focus on the historical development of organised crime in the country. Rather, three of those earlier studies focused on issues relating to gang organisation, drug distribution and childhood adversities more specifically. Thus, although there exists considerable overlap between those data sets and the one specific to the MRes, research questions inevitably differ and thus the framing of the question and response may be different, had they been framed to the topic in question here. Many of the participants in earlier studies, may have discussed the early developments of those gangs involved in, for example the Paisley drug wars, but the fact that the research question was not centred on this area, meant that chances to collect data specific to this, were ultimately missed, or is in many respects limited – rather being drawn out from other areas of discussion alluding back to issues of early gang reorganisation.

The limitations of the research of course go beyond those mentioned above, but again, the book's scope, and word length, among other restrictions, means that broader and more encompassed discussion of limitations are selected here, as opposed to being exhaustive. The research though does have a number of strengths which should be highlighted. Perhaps the most notable strength of the publication is that the book takes information given from official documentation, over a decade worth of fieldwork on the ground, and multiple autobiographical accounts from those involved in criminality, compiling them all into one chronological publication allowing those works to be explored, analysed and framed within a particular narrative for readers to understand the ebbs, flows and development of drug-based organised crime within the Scottish context. In addition, this allows for other comparable analysis with this particular case study to be compared to similar events in other UK localities, as well as those within an international context in some cases. Having a comparable analysis enables practitioners, stakeholders and policy makers in Scotland to compare organised crime in the country with their contemporaries and thus derive, and in some cases cherry-pick, from interventionist strategies and techniques utilised elsewhere, to be applied in the given context, in any effort to halt criminality. Furthermore, having a chronological source for the development of these criminal gangs can allow, albeit still limited, some degree of predictability regarding the ongoing and true development of these criminal groups, should mistakes be repeated, or their development left unchecked.

Future research, therefore, should seek to build upon the work outlined here. In doing so, the researchers would encourage others to challenge and rebut this particular research, in part, in order that alterative views and insights be offered up, adding to the value of this work and future research. This book should ideally act as a starting point for other scholars in the field to draw upon as a foundational piece, albeit with its flaws and limitations, to support alternative views, or to give strength to the proposed narrative. The researchers would encourage other research in the area to shed light on other developments during the timeframe set out by this piece of work, from other localities across the United Kingdom, in order to demonstrate how events in one locality may have significant impact on another, even if hundreds or thousands of miles apart. The case set out in this book can be used as a blueprint by others tasked with the investigation of case study analysis on various aspects of organised criminality. This will enable others to examine whether similar events unfolded elsewhere, demonstrated similar or differing factors and variables. It would also allow comparable analysis of results. The research can, and should be, used by practitioners and law enforcement in the development of their efforts to combat, halt and prevent organised criminality from taking grip in communities.

COMBATTING DRUG CRIME: POLICY LESSONS

Although this book has made clear that the development of drug-based organised crime in Scotland was in many ways symptomatic of powerful global forces, especially deindustrialisation and neoliberalism, its analysis should not be taken as purely deterministic. Organised crime taking root in communities is not inevitable, and policymakers at the global, national (including devolved in the Scottish case) and local government can exert agency, both at the margins when acting in isolation, and still more powerfully when working in genuine partnership across borders and lines of jurisdiction and institutional demarcation. What specific lessons might policymakers learn from the research related in this book?

Lessons for National/Devolved Government

- When devising and reviewing community empowerment (and related) laws and policies, take care to ensure that frameworks are created such that local communities are *genuinely* consulted on any changes affecting their neighbourhoods and their facilities.
- All new policies and draft laws should be written, revised and monitored in ways that 'mainstream' the need to guard against their potential abuse by organised crime groups.
- Best practice, experience and expertise should be sought both internationally and from across the British Isles when devising new laws and policies, to guard against opening 'backdoors' which organised crime groups might exploit.

Lessons for Local Government

- Community empowerment and contracting out of services should be undertaken in ways that mainstream vigilance against 'backdoors' that might be exploited by organised crime groups.
- 'Fit and proper person' (FPP) tests should be carried out on all named applicants on local authority contract bids *and* 'participation request' applicants.
- Wherever possible, FPP tests should include multi-agency consultation, i.e. to rule out organised crime groups working as 'silent partners' on superficially respectable bids.
- Community groups who are granted participation requests should be expected to publish annual audited accounts.

Note: It is recognised that people with criminal records can and have provided valuable services for their communities. The aim of the above 'lessons' is not to exclude these people, but to exert maximum reasonable scrutiny in the effort to prevent community groups, facilities and initiatives from being hijacked for criminal purposes. The FPP tests are used widely in other areas of Scottish and UK public and business life. See for example (HM Government, 2023)

CHAPTER SUMMARY

This chapter's purpose was threefold. The first part of this chapter seeks to bring the reader up to date, into the contemporary period, with the rise and fall of Scotland's Narcos. In doing so we pose the question, what next? Given that over the last 50 years or so, the country's criminal gangs have reorganised themselves specifically around a growing drugs trade, and in doing so have become increasingly sophisticated and resilient to external pressures, how should steps be implemented to halt the progress of these criminal groups? Surely the case study offered here suggests that, if unchecked, the next step would be for these groups to further exploit inroads into the political realm. In doing so, they would truly reflect the narratives which already surround those mafia style structures that exist in other European countries such as Italy and Russia. The second part of this chapter set out the strengths and limitations of the book, and in doing so seeks to encourage other scholars to use this piece as a blueprint for future research in the field. The third and final part of this chapter, before this summary, set out lessons from this book for local and national policymakers seeking to prevent organised crime groups from infiltrating national and local policies and subverting these to their nefarious advantage.

REFERENCES

Abrams, L. (2010). *Oral history theory* (2nd ed.). Routledge.

Albanese, J. S. (2014). *Organized crime: From the mob to transnational organized crime*. Taylor & Francis Group. ProQuest Ebook Central. http://ebookcentral.proquest.com/lib/open/detail.action?docID=1864814

Alexander, D. (2009, August 10). Exclusive: France's biggest ever drug haul was heading to Scotland. *Daily Record*.

Alexander, D. (2014, November 2). Revealed: Property and Taxi Tycoon meets drug baron and crime clan member. *Daily Record*.

Alexander, D. (2017, February 19). Ex-crime lord Grant Mackintosh says ex-RBS banker cousin is now the family black sheep. *Daily Record*.

Andell, P., & Pitts, J. (2018). The end of the line? The impact of county lines drug distribution on youth crime in a target destination. *Youth & Policy*. https://www.youthandpolicy.org/articles/the-end-of-the-line/

Barnes, T., Elias, R., & Walsh, P. (2011). *Cocky*. Milo Books Ltd.

Bartie, A. (2010). Moral panics and Glasgow gangs: Exploring the new wave into Glasgow hooliganism, 1965–1970. *Contemporary British History*, 24(3), 385–408.

Bauman, Z. (1989). *Modernity and the holocaust*. Polity Press.

BBC. (1993, July 4). On the record: Tony Blair interview. (Transcript from transmission). https://www.bbc.co.uk/otr/intext92-93/Blair4.7.93.html. Accessed on May 9.

BBC. (2015, March 25). Martin Toner murder trial: Widow 'knew' body found was husband. *BBC News*.

BBC. (2017, December 11). Scottish court hears of 'sophisticated' crime gang. *BBC News*.

BBC. (2018a, November 26). Derek Brockwell: 'Career criminal' wins sentence severity appeal. *BBC News*.

BBC. (2018b, January 22). The downfall of Scotland's most dangerous crime gang. *BBC News*.

BBC. (2018c, May 11). Gangster jailed over high-speed chase through Glasgow. *BBC News*.

BBC. (2019, May 9). Drug users in Scotland 'consume most cocaine' in one session. *BBC News*.

BBC. (2021, May 7). Hitman convicted of murdering T2 Trainspotting actor Bradley Welsh. *BBC News*.

BBC. (2022, March 4). Man jailed for murder of dad near Glasgow play park. *BBC News*.

BBC. (2023a, January 27). Fugitive Gillespie brothers may have been killed in Brazil. *BBC News*.

BBC. (2023b, August 11). Scots fugitive jailed for 10 years for drugs and gun offences. *BBC News*.

BBC iPlayer. (2023). *Ice cream wars*. BBC iPlayer.

BBC News. (1997). Low-key campaign in Paisley after Labour MP's suicide. Tuesday, November 4. http://news.bbc.co.uk/1/hi/special_report/paisley_by_election/19585.stm

BBC News. (2012, April 16). Kevin 'Gerbil' Carroll: Gangster 'killed in 25 seconds'. *BBC News*.

Boyle, J. (1977). *A sense of freedom*. Pan Books.

Black, D. C. (2020). *Review of drugs – Evidence relating to drug use, supply and effects, including current trends and future risks*. Home Office, UK government.

Bramley-Harker, E. (2001). *Sizing the UK market for illicit drugs*. US department of Justice.

Broadhurst, R., & Wa, L. K. (2009). The transformation of Triad "Dark Societies" in Hong Kong: The impact of law enforcement, socio-economic and political change. *Security Challenges*, 5(4), 1–38.

Campana, P., & Varese, F. (2018). Organized crime in the United Kingdom: Illegal governance of markets and communities. *British Journal of Criminology*, 58(6), 1381–1400. https://doi.org/10.1093/bjc/azx078

Campana, P., & Varese, F. (2020). Studying organized crime networks: Data sources, boundaries and the limits of structural measures. *Social Networks*, 69, 149–159.

Casey, J., Hay, G., Godfrey, C., & Parrot, S. (2009). *Assessing the scale and impact of illicit drug Markets in Scotland*. Scottish Government.

Census. (2022). *Rounded population estimates*. Scottish Government.

Clark, A. (2021). 'There is nothing there for us and nothing for the future': Deindustrialization and workplace occupation, 1981–1982. *Labour History Review*, 86(1), 37–61.

Clark, A. (2023). 'People just dae wit they can tae get by': Exploring the half-life of deindustrialisation in a Scottish community. *The Sociological Review*, 71(2), 332–350.

Clark, A., & Gibbs, E. (2020). Voices of social dislocation, lost work and economic restructuring: Narratives from marginalised localities in the 'New Scotland'. *Memory Studies*, 13(1), 39–59.

Collins, C. (1999). Applying Bakhtin in urban studies: The failure of community participation in the Ferguslie Park partnership. *Urban Studies*, 35(1), 73–90.

Coomber, R. (2006). *Pusher myths: Re-situating the drug dealer*. Free Association Books.

Crocker, R., Webb, S., Skidmore, M., Garner, S., Gill, M., & Graham, J. (2019). Tackling local organised crime groups: Lessons from research in two UK cities. *Trends in Organised Crime*, 22, 433–449.

Cullen, D. (1996). *Public inquiry into the shootings at Dunblane Primary School*. HM Government.

Daily Record. (1996, August 21). Gun gangster gets 6 years for pinching Lion King cake; M&S guard threatened. *Daily Record*.

Daily Record. (1999, December 15). Suspect in killing gunned down outside nightclub. *Daily Record*.

Daily Record. (2003, July 2). 9 Murders linked to Costa Crook. *Daily Record*.

Damer, S. (2018). *A social history of Glasgow Council Housing, 1919-1956*. Edinburgh University Press.

Davies, A. (1998). Street gangs, crime and policing in Glasgow during the 1930s: The case of the Beehive Boys. *Social History*, 23(3), 251–267.

Davies, A. (2013). *City of gangs: Glasgow and the rise of the British gangster*. Hodder & Stoughton.

Dean, H., & Platt, L. (2016). *Social advantage and disadvantage*. Oxford University Press.

Densley, J., McLean, R., & Brick, C. (2022). *Contesting county lines: Case studies in drug crime and criminal entrepreneurialism*. Springer Publishing.

Densley, J., McLean, R., Deuchar, R., & Harding, S. (2018). An altered state? Emergent changes to illicit drug markets and distribution networks in Scotland. *International Journal of Drug Policy, 58*, 113–120.

Densley, J., McLean, R., Deuchar, R., & Harding, S. (2019). Progression from cafeteria to à la carte offending: Scottish organised crime narratives. *Howard Journal of Crime and Justice*. https://doi.org/10.1111/hojo.12304

Deuchar, R. (2013). *Policing youth violence: Transatlantic connections*. Trentham/IOE.

Deuchar, R., McLean, R., Harding, S., & Densley, J. (2020). Deficit or credit? A comparative, qualitative study of gender agency and female gang membership in Los Angeles and Glasgow. *Crime & Delinquency*. https://doi.org/10.1177/0011128718794192

Deuchar, R., McLean, R., & Holligan, C. (2021). *Gangs, drugs and youth adversity*. Bristol University Press.

Dickie, J. (2007). *Cosa Nostra: The definitive history of the Sicilian mafia*. Hodder.

Dickie, J. (2012). *Mafia brotherhoods: Camorra, mafia, 'ndrangheta: The rise of the honoured societies*. Hodder.

Documentary City. (2022, July 14). *Glasgow's drug war - the Lyons vs the Daniels - Scottish gangland documentary*. YouTube.

EMCDDA. (2019). *European drug report 2019*. European Monitoring Centre for Drugs and Drug Addiction.

Farrington, D., Coid, J., Harnett, L., Jolliffe, D., Soteriou, N., Turner, R., & West, D. (2006). *Criminal careers and life success*. Home Office.

Ferlie, E. (2017, March 29). The new public management and public management studies. In *Oxford research encyclopaedia of business and management*. https://oxfordre.com/business/view/10.1093/acrefore/

9780190224851.001.0001/acrefore-9780190224851-e-129. Accessed on January 15, 2024.

Ferris, P. (2005). *Vandetta: Turning your back on crime can be deadly*. Black and White Publishing Limited.

Ferris, P., & McKay, R. (2001). *The Ferris Conspiracies*. Black and White Publishing Limited.

Ferris, P., & McKay, R. (2002). *Deadly divisions: The spectre chronicles*. Black and White Publishing Limited.

Ferris, P., & McKay, R. (2010). *Villains: It takes one to know one*. Black and White Publishing Limited.

Findlay, R. (2008). *The Iceman: The rise and fall of a crime lord*. Barlinn Limited.

Findlay, R. (2010, January 17). Crime clan godfather vows bloody revenge for slain hoodlum at secret summit. *Sunday Mail*.

Findlay, R. (2012a). *Caught in the crossfire: Scotland's deadliest drugs war*. Birlinn Limited.

Findlay, R. (2012b, June 24). Searing new book lifts lid on the bitter gangland war between the Daniel and Lyons crime clans. *Daily Record*.

Findlay, R. (2018a). *Acid attack: A journalist's war with organised crime*. Barlinn Limited.

Findlay, R. (2018b, May 29). The Lyons v the Daniels, politics, Glasgow City Council and the shooting that stunned a city. *Glasgow Live*.

Findlay, R. (2018c, May 28). Chirnsyde and the Lyons v Daniels, how a youth club became a playground for Glasgow's most notorious gang war. *Glasgow Live*.

Galeotti, M. (2018). *The vory*. Yale University Press.

Gibbs, E. (2018). The moral economy of the Scottish coalfields: Managing deindustrialization under nationalization c.1947–1983. *Enterprise and Society*, 19(1), 124–152.

Gibbs, E. (2021). *Coal country: The meaning and memory of deindustrialization in Postwar Scotland*. Series: New historical perspectives. University of London Press.

Gilmour, A. (2007). The trouble with Linwood: Compliance and Coercion in the car plant, 1963–1981, *Journal of Scottish Historical Studies*, 27(1), 75–93.

Giommoni, L., Gundur, R. V., & Cheekes, E. (2020). International drug trafficking: Past, present, and prospective trends. In *Oxford research encyclopedia of criminology and criminal justice*. OUP.

Gootenburg, P. (2012). *Cocaine's 'Blowback' north: A commodity chain pre-history of the Mexican drug crisis*. JSTOR.

Gray, A. (1989). *A history of Scotland: Modern times*. Oxford University Press.

Gun Control Network. (2024). US UK comparative data. https://gun-control-network.org. Accessed on May 7.

Gundur, R. (2022). *Trying to Make It: The Enterprises, Gangs, and People of the American Drug Trade*. Cornell University Press. NY.

Hales, G., & Hobbs, D. (2010). Drug markets in the community: a London borough case study. *Trends in Organised Crime, 3*, 13–30.

Hallsworth, S., & Young, T. (2008). Gang talk & gang talkers: A critique. *Crime, Media, Culture, 4*, 175–195.

Handley, J. E. (1950). The position of catholics in social and economic history. *The Innes Review*, 1(2), 100.

Handley, J. E. (2001). *Irish in Scotland*. Cork University Press.

Harding, S. (2020). *County lines: Exploitation and drug dealing among urban street gangs*. Bristol University Press.

Harding, S., Deuchar, R., Densley, J., & McLean, R. (2019). A typology of street robbery and gang organization: Insights from qualitative research in Scotland. *British Journal of Criminology*. https://doi.org/10.1093/bjc/azy064

HM Advocate. (2022, July 27). James Scott McDonald & Raymond Anderson v Her Majesty Advocate, p. 9.

HM Government. (2023). The fit and proper test. https://www.gov.uk/guidance/money-laundering-regulations-apply-for-the-fit-and-proper-test. Accessed on May 10, 2024.

Hobbs, D. (2013). *Lush life: Constructing organised crime in the UK*. Oxford University Press.

Hobbs, D., & Antonopoulos, G. A. (2013a). 'Endemic to the species': Ordering the 'other' via organised crime. *Global Crime, 14*, 27–51.

Hobbs, D., & Antonopoulos, G. A. (2013b). How to research organised crime. In L. Paoli (Ed.), *The Oxford handbook of organized crime*. Oxford University Press.

Holligan, C., McLean, R., & Deuchar, R. (2016). Don't you know Glasgow's the stab capital of the world? Understanding the narratives about weapon carrying among working-class teenage boys in Glasgow. *Critical Criminology, 25*(1), 137–151.

Holligan, C., McLean, R., & McHugh, R. (2020). Venturing capitalism: Exploring county lines drug distribution in Scotland. *Journal of Youth Studies*. Special Issue: Street Gangs, Group Offending and Violence. https://doi.org/10.1177/1473225420902850

Holligan, C., McLean, R., & Rice, G. (2019). Scotland's drug criminality: Organised crime group (s) and illegal governance. *Deviant Behaviour*. https://doi.org/10.1080/01639625.2019.1697417

Jeffery, R. (2011). *Glasgow's godfather: The astonishing inside story of Walter Norval, the city's first crime boss*. Black & White Publishing.

Johnson, G. (2007). *The Devil: Britain's most feared underworld taxman*. Mainstream Publishing.

Kaplan, D. E., & Dubro, A. (2012). *Yakuza: Japan's criminal underworld*. University of California Press.

Katz, J. (1988). *Seductions of crime*. Basic Books.

Kefauver, E. C. (1951). *Special Committee on organized crime in interstate commerce*. Resolution passed May 2nd. https://stoppredatorygambling.org/wp-content/uploads/2012/12/Kefauver-Committee-Final-report.pdf

Kennedy, C. (2018). *Vengeance, violence, and vigilantism: An exploration of the 1891 lynching of eleven Italian-Americans in New Orleans* (Vol. 149). Honors Theses. University of Mississippi. https://egrove.olemiss.edu/hon_thesis/149

Kirby, S., & Nailor, L. (2013). Reducing the offending of a UK organized crime group using an opportunity-reducing framework—A three-year case study. *Trends in Organised Crime, 16*, 397–412.

Lambert, T. (2023). *A history of Glasgow*. Local Histories. https://localhistories.org/a-history-of-glasgow/. Accessed on September 11, 2023.

Levi, M. (2016). Thinking about organised crime structure and threat. *The RUSI Journal, 159*(1), 6–14.

Lombardo, R. M. (2013). Fighting organized crime: A history of law enforcement efforts in Chicago. *Journal of Contemporary Criminal Justice*, 29(2), 296–316.

MacDonald, C. (2011, September 1). The Radical Thread - Liberalism and the rise of Labour in Scotland 1886 - 1924. *Mémoire(s), identité(s), marginalité(s) dans le monde occidental contemporain*. https://doi.org/10.4000/mimmoc.681

Mares, D. (1999). Globalization and gangs: The Manchester case. *Foccal*, 35, 135–155.

Matza, D. (1964). *Delinquency and drift*. Prentice-Hall.

May, T., & Hough, M. (2001). Drug markets and distribution systems. *Addiction Research and Theory*, 12(6), 549–563.

McAlpine, J. (2006, December 17). This is a nasty stink you cannot just ignore, Jack. *The Times*.

McCabe, G. (2017, December 11). Torture gang broke victim's leg, shot him three times, doused him in bleach and rolled him naked down a hill. *Daily Record*.

McCabe, G. (2022, March 4). Scots fugitive Jordan Owens jailed for murder of Glasgow playpark victim Jamie Lee. *Daily Record*.

McGivern, M. (2016, July 5). Death of ruthless gangland boss Jamie Daniel will mark the end of Scottish crime clan era. *Daily Record*.

McGivern, M. (2018, November 28). See inside Paisley 'Breaking Bad' pill factory after 'Blue Plague' gang busted. *Daily Record*.

McIvor, A., & Johnston, R. (2004). Dangerous work, hard men and broken bodies: Masculinity in the clydeside heavy industries. *Labour History Review*, 69(2), 135–152.

McKay, R. (2002). *Armed Candy: A true-life story of organised crime*. Black and White Publishing Limited.

McKay, R. (2006a). *Murder Capital: Life and death on the streets of Glasgow*. Black and White Publishing Limited.

McKay, R. (2006b). *The last godfather: The life and crimes of Arthur Thompson*. Black and White Publishing.

McKay, R. (2007). *The last godfather: The life and crimes of Arthur Thompson*. Black and White Publishing Limited.

McKay, R. (2010). *McGraw: The untold story of Tam 'The License' McGraw*. Black and White Publishing Limited.

McKay, R. (2017, May 18). *The Lyons v the Daniels, the incredible inside story of Glasgow's gang wars*. GlasgowLive.

McLean, R. (2017). An evolving gang model in contemporary Scotland. *Deviant Behavior*. https://doi.org/10.1080/01639625.2016.1272969

McLean, R. (2018). *Discovering young crime gangs in Glasgow. Gang organisation as a means for gang business*. Unpublished doctoral thesis. University of the West of Scotland.

McLean, R. (2019a). *Gangs, drugs and disorganised crime*. Bristol University Press.

McLean, R. (2019b). Glasgow's evolving urban landscape and gang formation. *Deviant Behavior, 40*(5), 498–509.

McLean, R. (2024). *Change and continuality: A contemporary history of drug-based organised crime in the west of Scotland since the 1980s*. Unpublished thesis. Strathclyde University.

McLean, R., Holligan, C., & McPhee, I. (2017). Market testing and market policing: Illuminating the fluid micro-sociology of the illegal drug supply enterprise in liquid modernity. *Deviant Behaviour, 40*(5), 485–497.

McLean, R., Deuchar, R., Harding, S., & Densley, J. (2019a). Putting the 'Street' in gang: Place and space in the organisation of Scotland's drug selling gangs. *British Journal of Criminology*. https://doi.org/10.1093/bjc/azy015

McLean, R., Robinson, G., & Densley, J. (2019b). *County Lines: Criminal networks and evolving drug markets in Britain*. Springer Publishers.

McPhee, I. (2013). *The intentionally unseen: Illicit & illegal drug use in Scotland: Exploring 'drug talk' in The 21st century*. Lambert University Publishers.

McPhee, I., McLean, R., Deuchar, R., & Holligan, C. (2019). Dr Jekyll and Mr Hyde: The strange case of the two selves of clandestine drug users in Scotland. *Drugs and Alcohol Today, 19*(2), 133–146.

McSweeney, T., Turnbull, P., & Hough, M. (2008). *Tackling drug markets and distribution networks in the UK: A review of the recent literature*. UKPDC.

Miller, J. (2015). *In every scheme there is a team: A grounded theory of how young people grow in and out of gangs in Glasgow*. Unpublished Thesis. University West of Scotland.

Morselli, C. (2003). Career opportunities and network-based privileges in the Cosa Nostra. *Crime Law Society Change*, 39(4), 383–418.

Moyle, L., & Coomber, R. (2015). Earning a score: An exploration of the nature and roles of heroin and crack cocaine user-dealers. *British Journal of Criminology*, 55(3), 534–555.

Mulholland, J. (2021, March 5). Scots gangsters lose freedom appeal bid after claim jury 'made their mind up'. *Daily Record*.

Murray, C. (1984). *Losing ground: American social policy 1950–1980*. Basic Books.

National Crime Agency (NCA). (2013). *Serious organised crime strategy*. Home Office and HM Government.

National Crime Agency (NCA). (2020). *NCA and police smash thousands of criminal conspiracies after infiltration of encrypted communication platform in UK's biggest ever law enforcement operation*. National Crime Agency.

National Records of Scotland. (2023). *Drug-related deaths in Scotland in 2022*. Scottish Government.

National Society for the prevention of Cruelty to Children (NSPCC). (2023, July 12). Protecting children from county lines. https://learning.nspcc.org.uk/child-abuse-and-neglect/county-lines#:~:text=County%20lines%20is%20a%20form%20of%20criminal%20exploitation,the%20law%20and%20a%20form%20of%20child%20abuse. Accessed on November 03, 2023.

New York Times. (1993, August 15). War on organized crime. *New York Times*, 1.

O'Mahoney, B. (2003). *Essex boys: A terrifying expose of the British drugs scene*. Transworld Publishers.

Paisley Daily Express. (2021, May 29). Crime clan thug caged for raping young girls. https://www.dailyrecord.co.uk/news/local-news/crime-clan-thug-jailed-raping-24210204

Panorama. (1996). *Drug rule*. BBC Documentaries.

Parker, H. (2000). How young Britons obtain their drugs: Drugs transactions at the point of consumption. In M. Hough & M. Natarajan (Eds.), *Illegal drug markets: From research to prevention policy*. Criminal Justice Press.

Parker, H., Bury, C., & Egginton, R. (1998). *New heroin outbreaks amongst young people in England and Wales*. Home Office.

Paterson, K. (2022, September 14). Liz Truss & Paisley: The town that made a prime minister. *Holyrood*. https://www.holyrood.com/news/view,liz-truss-paisley-the-town-the-made-a-prime-minister. Accessed on May 7, 2024.

Pearson, J., & Hobbs, D. (2001). *Middle market drug distribution*. Home Office.

Peniston-Bird, C. (2008). *Oral history: The sound of memory*. Routledge.

Phillips, J., Wright, V., & Tomlinson, J. (2019). Being a 'Clydesider' in the age of deindustrialisation: Skilled male identity and economic restructuring in the West of Scotland since the 1960s. *Labor History, 61*(2), 151–156.

Picarelli, J. T. (2012). Osama bin Corleone? Vito the Jackal? Framing threat convergence through an examination of transnational organized crime and international terrorism. *Terrorism and Political Violence, 24*(2), 180–198.

Pitts, J. (2008). *Reluctant gangsters: The changing face of youth crime*. Routledge.

Plummer, K. (2001). *Documents of life: An invitation to a critical humanism*. Sage.

Pudney, S., Badillo, C., Bryan, M., Burton, J., Conti, G., & Iacovou, M. (2006). Estimating the size of the UK illicit drug market. In N. Singleton, R. Murray, & L. Tinsley (Eds.), *Measuring different aspects of problem drug use: Methodological developments*. Home Office.

Pugh, M. (2014, June). Centralism versus localism? Democracy versus efficiency? The perennial challenges of Scottish local government organisation. *History and Policy*.

Pugh, M. (2016). Civic borders and imagined communities: Continuity and change in Scotland's municipal boundaries, jurisdictions and structures - From nineteenth-century "General police" to twenty first-century "community empowerment". *Études Écossaises, 18*, 29–49.

Pugh, M., & Connolly, J. (2014, September 5). *Written submission to Scottish Government on draft community empowerment bill*. National Records of Scotland.

Pugh, M., & Connolly, J. (2016). A review of contemporary linked challenges for Scottish local government. *Scottish Affairs*, 25(3), 317–336.

Rafanell, I., Mclean, R., & Poole, L. (2017). Emotions and hyper-masculine subjectivities: The role of affective sanctioning in Glasgow gangs. *NORMA: International Journal for Masculinity Studies*. https://doi.org/10.1080/18902138.2017.1312958

Rahman, M., McLean, R., Deuchar, R., & Densley, J. (2022). Who are the enforcers? The motives and methods of muscle for hire in West Scotland and the West Midlands. *Trends in Organized Crime*, 1–22.

Rannoc, T. (2019). *Van Wars: The real story of the brutal Glasgow Ice-Cream Van Wars*. Independently Published.

Rege, A. (2016). Not biting the dust: Using a tripartite model of organized crime to examine India's Sand Mafia. *International Journal of Comparative and Applied Criminal Justice*, 40(2), 101–121.

Reinarman, C. (1979). Moral entrepreneurs and political economy: Historical and ethnographic notes on the construction of the cocaine menace. *Contemporary Crises*, 3, 225–254.

Renfrewshire Council. (2014). Paisley, the untold story: Paisley Town Centre Asset Strategy & Action Plan. https://www.renfrewshire.gov.uk/media/2088/Paisley-The-Untold-Story/pdf/PaisleyUntoldStory.pdf?m=1460044670430. Accessed on May 7, 2020.

Reuter, P., & Greenfield, V. (2001). Measuring global drug markets: How good are the numbers and why should we care about them? *World Economics*, 2(4), 159–173.

Reynolds, G. (2020). *'County lines' in the countryside: Exploring the extent of out- of-county drug dealing in the county of Cumbria*. Unpublished thesis. University of Lancaster.

Rhodes, R. A. W. (1994). The hollowing out of the local state: The changing nature of the public service in Britain. *The Political Quarterly*, 65(2), 138–151.

Robertson, I. (1984). Single parent lifestyle and peripheral estate residence: A time-geographic investigation in Drumchapel, Glasgow. *The Town Planning Review*, 55, 197–213.

Robinson, G., McLean, R., & Densley, J. (2019). Working county lines: Child criminal exploitation and illicit drug dealing in Glasgow and Merseyside.

International Journal of Offender Therapy and Comparative Criminology, 63(5), 1–18.

Ruggiero, V. (2010). Unintended consequences: Changes in organised drug supply in the UK. *Trends in Organized Crime, 13*, 46–59.

Scott, J., & Hughes, M. (1980). *The anatomy of Scottish capital: Scottish companies and Scottish capital, 1900–1979.* Routledge.

Scottish Courts & Tribunals. (1986, August 1). McIntosh v HM Advocate, High Court of Judiciary, *169*(29). Ross, Lords Robertson, Sutherland.

Scottish Courts & Tribunals. (2011). McDonald J. S & Anderson R v Her Majesty Advocate, Court of Appeal, Criminal division, case 319/08.

Scottish Courts & Tribunals. (2022a). McDonald J. S. & Anderson R v Her Majesty Advocate, Court of Appeal, Criminal division, case 319/08.

Scottish Courts & Tribunals. (2022b). McDonald J. S. & Anderson R v Her Majesty Advocate, 07/27/2022, P1-32.

Scottish Government. (2008). *The road to recovery: A new approach to tackling Scotland's drug problem.* Scottish Government.

Scottish Government. (2009). *Letting our communities flourish: A strategy for tackling serious organised crime in Scotland.* Scottish Government.

Scottish Government. (2015). *Scotland serious organised crime strategy.* Scottish Government.

Scottish Government. (2016). *Scotland serious organised crime strategy annual review.* Scottish Government.

Scottish Government. (2023). *Suspected drug deaths in Scotland.* Scottish Government.

Segel, G. M. (2010). Is the UK stepping toward transnationalism? The serious organized crime agency. In E. Aydinli (Ed.), *Emerging transnational (in) security governance: A statist-transnationalist approach* (pp. 84–101). Taylor & Francis Group.

Sergi, A. (2015). Divergent mind-sets, convergent policies: Policing models against organized crime in Italy and in England within international frameworks. *European Journal of Criminology, 12*(6), 658–680.

Shapiro, H. (2021). *Fierce chemistry: A history of UK drug wars.* Amberley Publishing.

Shapiro, J., & Siegel, D. (2012). Moral hazard, discipline, and the management of terrorist organizations. *World Politics, 64*.

Shelley, L. I., & Picarelli, J. T. (2005). Methods and motives: Exploring links between transnational organized crime and international terrorism. *Trends in Organized Crime, 9*, 52–67. https://doi.org/10.1007/s12117-005-1024-x

Sillitoe, P. (1956). *Cloak without dagger*. Cassell.

Silvester, N. (2021, November 3). The Glasgow crime story of the murder of Martin Toner. *Glasgow Times*.

Silvester, N. (2022, November 21). Glasgow crime story of gangland figure murder 'The Gerbil'. *GlasgowLive*.

Silvester, N. (2023, February 19). The Glasgow crime story of Jamie Daniel. *Daily Record*.

Sims, E. W. (1920). Fighting crime in Chicago: The crime commission. *Journal of the American Institute of Criminal Law and Criminology, 11*(1), 21–28.

Sky. (2020, July 3). EncroChat: What it is, who was running it, and how did criminals get their encrypted phones? *Sky News*.

Smolíková, S., & Smolík, J. (2011). Actors of Columbian drug trade : Development and transformation. *Obrana a Strategie*, (1), 053–068.

Snelders, S. (2021). *Drug smuggler nation: Narcotics and The Netherlands, 1920–1995*. Manchester University Press.

Squires, P. (2000). *Gun culture or gun control? Firearms and violence: Safety and society*. Routledge.

Squires, P., Silvestri, A., Grimshaw, R., & Solomon, E. (2008). *Street weapons commission: Guns, knives and street violence*. Centre for Crime and Justice Studies.

Sunday Time. (2006, December 17). This is a nasty stink you cannot just ignore, Jack'.

Sutherland, E. (1937). *The professional thief*. University of Chicago Press.

The Herald. (1993a, September 28). Man jailed on drugs charge.

The Herald. (1993b, December 8). Courier trapped with drugs worth £400,000 is jailed.

The Herald. (1993c, February 20). Murder trial adjourned.

The Herald. (1994a, March 16). Second man accused.

References

The Herald. (1994b, March 16). Mans murder might have been revenge killing.

The Herald. (1995a, March 29). Man who survived earlier shooting may have been lured to his death in Glasgow. The drug war killing field widens.

The Herald. (1995c, March 18). Police turn up heat on drugs and guns.

The Herald. (1995d, April 29). Man in court charged with murder attempts.

The Herald. (1995e, October 3). Two jailed for Paisley shootings.

The Herald. (1995f, April 11). Man accused.

The Herald. (1995g, March 16). Crime count that wont add up.

The Herald. (1995h, June 23). Newspaper not intimidated by fire-bomb.

The Herald. (1995i, July 28). Mother in appeal to find killer.

The Herald. (1996a, October 19). Business set up to revitalise Ferguslie Park has itself been accused of criminal activity estate that is also a battleground.

The Herald. (1996b, May 25). Gang fears mount in wake of gun death.

The Herald. (1997, August 13). Jury clears man over gangland execution.

The Herald. (2003, October 16). 70 years and apos; jail for gang who killed the wrong man.

The Herald. (2017, December 10). The Celtic skipper, the drug dealer gunman, and the gang of nine.

The Herald. (2019, April 28). Lyons and Daniels - inside a very Scottish gang feud.

The Urban Historian. (2018, August 7). The "Newshot", Fleming & Ferguson, Paisley 1943'. https://www.theurbanhistorian.co.uk/the-newshot-fleming-ferguson-paisley-1943/. Accessed on May 7, 2024.

Thrasher, F. (1927). *A study of 1,313 gangs in Chicago*. Chicago University Press.

UK Parliament. (2006, February 27). Scottish National Party victory in Milton by-election. https://edm.parliament.uk/early-day-motion/30140/scottish-national-party-victory-in-milton-byelection

United Nations Office on Drugs and Crime (UNODC). (2005). *World drug report 2005*. United Nations. https://www.unodc.org/pdf/WDR_2005/volume_1_web.pdf

United Nation on Drug and Crime (UNODC). (2021). *World drug report*. United Nation.

United States Supreme Court. (2008). District of Columbia v. Heller, 554 U.S. 570.

Von Lampe, K. (2016). *Organized crime*. Sage.

Wacquant, L. (2000). Deadly symbiosis: When Ghetto and prison meet and mesh. *Sage Journals, 3*(1).

Wacquant, L. (2008). *Urban outcasts: A comparative sociology of advanced marginality*. Polity.

Wacquant, L. (2010). Crafting the neoliberal state: Workfare, prison fare and social security. *Sociological Fourm, 25*(2), 197–220.

Wagstaff, A., & Maynard, A. (1988). *Economic aspects of the illicit drug market and drug enforcement policies in the United Kingdom*. HM Government.

Walker, A. (2022, July 25). Glasgow gangster Robert Daniel jailed after DNA found at crime scene. *Scottish Sun*.

Walsh, D., Bendel, N., Jones, R., & Hanlon, P. (2010). *Investigating a 'Glasgow Effect' Why do equally deprived UK cities experience different health outcomes?* Glasgow Centre for Population Health.

Williams, R. (1994). Medical, economic and population factors in areas of high mortality: The case of Glasgow. *Sociology of Health & Illness, 16*(2).

Wilson, C. (2024, April 23). Trading crime for culture? Activating territorial stigma through cultural regeneration in Paisley. *Urban Geography*. https://doi.org/10.1080/02723638.2024.2333698

Wilson, J. Q., & Hernstein, R. (1985). *Crime and human nature*. Simon and Schuster.

Windle, J. (2013). Tuckers firm: A case study of British organised crime. *Trends in Organised Crime, 16*, 382–396.

Windle, J., & Briggs, D. (2015). 'It's like working away for two weeks': The harms associated with young drug dealers commuting from a saturated London drug market. *Crime Prevention and Community Safety, 17*(2), 105–119.

Wright, V. (2018). Tinkering at a local level: Unemployment, state intervention and community agency in Ferguslie Park, Paisley c. 1972–1977. *Scottish Labour History, 53*, 192–211.

Printed and bound by CPI Group (UK) Ltd, Croydon, CR0 4YY
23/09/2024

14562156-0002